PUBERTY DROVE THE CAR:

I was just along for the ride

Scott Eubanks

STEPHEN F. AUSTIN STATE UNIVERSITY PRESS

Copyright © 2020 by Stephen F. Austin University Press

All rights reserved
First Edition
Printed in United States of America

For information about permission to reproduce selections from this book, contact *permissions* :

Stephen F. Austin State University Press
P.O. Box 13007, SFA Station
Nacogdoches, TX 75962
sfapress@sfasu.edu
www.sfasu.edu/sfapress
936-468-1078

ISBN: 978-1-62288-309-7

Edited and designed by: Jakayla Murphy
Cover Art: Tristan Brewster

The views and opinions expressed in this book are the authors's own and do not reflect the views and opinions of Stephen F. Austin State University, its Board of Regents, or the State of Texas.

We all grow up with heroes. I did. In my first book, *Mad Dogs, Marbles, and Rock Fights*, I saluted four female heroes: my mother, two aunts, and a teacher. It seems only fair that in my second book I pay written homage to my three male heroes.

My dad, Homer Eubanks, and my older brothers, Homer, Jr., and Robert, all spent considerable time teaching me, molding me, correcting me, guiding me, and just plain loving me. Daddy worked hard and lovingly on instilling in me the values of honesty, compassion, character, loyalty, and a toughness that still gives me strength when I face adversity. Daddy also planted the seeds of optimism deep inside of me that took root and have marched me through life with a confidence that few others have enjoyed.

Homer and Robert were ideal big brothers. Even though they were thirteen and ten years older than me, they always took time to include me in many of their activities. Their friends were my friends. They were both big, strong, athletic boys, and their mere existence kept the bullies away. No one messed with me, fearing they would suffer the wrath of my two protective, loving brothers. Even in adulthood, I have enjoyed walking in the comfort of their shadows. I always admired my brothers and, in case you didn't pick-up on it, I loved them fiercely.

TABLE OF CONTENTS

Introduction   7

The Marshall, Texas I Knew   9

The First Day of Junior High or, Unbridled Confusion   15

A Comb, a Butt Kicking, and Communal Showers   18

Puberty: Guilt, Fustration, Passion, Insanity, Etc.   27

The Spotlight on Big Time Junior High Sports   34

Learning how to Cuss   42

Be Still My Heart   45

God, May I have Gravy with my Manna?   54

Never the Hero, Often the Goat   57

Bovine Diarrhea, and Stampeding Turkeys   64

Friends: Old and New   76

Mrs. Jones Had an Affair with A Fairy   82

An East Texas Ménage à Trois   92

Neely's on Grand   97

From Corvettes to the White Flash   102

The Bob Hope Motel, Bouree, and Cajun Baseball   111

TV, Elvis, Hairspray, and English Leather   122

A Hodgepodge of Unrealted Stories   128

And Then It Was Over   137

Acknowledgments   139

Introduction

My first book, *Mad Dogs, Marbles, and Rock Rights,* was a humorous look at my early years and the projects, situations, and predicaments my friends and I survived. It ended with us finishing our elementary school years. That summer between elementary school and junior high was a summer during which we became aware of some of the changes that were beginning to affect us and those that would soon alter our lives. The maturation of the girls in our lives was beginning to take shape, and there were stirrings in our bodies we clearly didn't understand. We boys knew the emergence of booblets, perfume, make-up, shaved legs, and some other stuff caused these strange stirrings, and it became apparent in junior high and, of course, high school was about to hit us like a ton of bricks. It did, and the main culprit was a monster called puberty. Yikes. This book picks up where *Mad Dogs, Marbles, and Rock Rights* left off. Both books are nostalgic and written to freeze a moment in time that was rich with fun, love, mistakes, hijinks, and youthful oddities. Don't let my mention of puberty mislead you. This book is not filled with juicy sex stuff, although there are hints of it. There was too much confusion over sex during those tender years for those stories to be included in a romance novel. It's a book about our sometimes clumsy and often funny march toward adulthood.

I once read, "We can't retire to the past, or even linger there for long as it can gray-down one's vision." While that warning has a ring of truth, I'm not totally convinced of its accuracy. I'm inclined to think it was said by someone whose early years were missing something. I also once read, "Nostalgia is an understandable response to a world that seems hellbent on destroying itself." I understand why folks sometimes feel like retreating from the frantic pace of today's lifestyle. Things move so fast these days, and many have become stingy with kind words. Now that I am in my 70s, I sometimes seek the refuge my happy past offers. I like to let treasured friends in my front door while shooing enemies and foes out my back door. You see, I loved my early years and my teen years spent growing up in Marshall, Texas. Good people of solid character surrounded me, and I take solace calling them to mind from deep inside my memory. I did things in those days I wish I hadn't done, but I have no reason to run from my past. I, instead, enjoy running toward it.

At the time of this writing, I read England had created a government Department of Loneliness to deal with the isolationism that runs rampant within Great Britain. Tragically, the loneliness in today's world is of epidemic proportions. I, perhaps naively, think that if all those lonely people had grown up in Marshall, Texas, in the late 1950s and early 1960s, they would never have known enduring loneliness. Marshall and its citizens nurtured us, loved us, and gave us a home to which we could always return. Maybe those were just days when people spared the time to show more care for other people than many do today. The 1950s and 1960s had a gentility and simplicity conducive to storing away good memories and enjoying your friends.

I have stuck pretty close to the truth in this book, and the characters are real. Granted, because of my age, my memory probably isn't as sharp as it once was. Even I don't trust it as much as I once did. However, I am counting on the memories of my classmates being even rustier than mine is, making it impossible for them to challenge me with conviction. Also, the older I've become, the more comfortable I've become with exaggeration. If you read this book and are tempted to correct my memory, please don't. I'm very sensitive.

There were quite a few other stories I could have included, and some great sex scenes I felt wise to omit. There were more almost-sex scenes, entertaining but incriminating, embarrassing moments I could have told on old friends but refrained from sharing lest I lose their trust. I also tried to avoid hurting or embarrassing anyone in these pages, not because I'm such a nice guy but to avoid lawsuits, angry husbands, wives, and murder. If I ever move to an isolated mountain cabin and vow never to return to civilization, I will write a tell-all scorcher. In the meantime, relax friends. Your secrets are safe with me.

Scott Eubanks

Chapter 01

The Marshall, Texas I Knew

The stories you are about to read took place in my hometown of Marshall, Texas, in the late 1950s and early 1960s. Those were my junior and senior high school years. I think knowing a little bit about Marshall helps to put those stories in better context. Marshall had an impressive, intriguing, and interesting history dating back to its founding in 1842. While tempted to do so, I will not use these pages to teach a history lesson, I will, however, recite a few facts that will give you a sense of what made Marshall tick.

Marshall and most of East Texas is heavily forested. Even the most avid arborist in the world could have spent most of his life categorizing the trees and other abundant flora of East Texas. Growing up, I remember the area as having mostly pines and oaks and, in fact, Marshall is slap-dab in the center of what is called the Piney Woods. Marshall receives 47 inches of rain per year, so its landscape is generally green and lush. It is also blessed with lots of lakes, rivers, streams, and ponds. The most famous body of water in Harrison County has always been the picturesque and somewhat mysterious Caddo Lake. Caddo is the only natural lake in Texas and the largest natural lake in the South.

Norman Rockwell could have spent his entire professional life in Marshall, Texas, in the 1950s and '60s, artistically capturing his glimpses into the lovable side of small-town America. Like so many other towns and small cities across our nation at that time, Marshall was still riding the wave of post-war prosperity. Its downtown streets were busy, its sidewalks crowded, and there were few, if any, vacant storefronts. Our fathers all had jobs if they wanted them. Oh, we had our poor, to be sure, but there was a palpable air of confidence and optimism that rippled through our town. It seemed to me Marshall sort of danced on the edge of a naïvete that signaled all was right with our world.

One scene I took in during my junior high days seemed to illustrate that sentiment best. I remember looking down toward Charlie Starke's house and seeing his high-school-aged brother, Ebb, working on the Model T Ford he and his dad had rebuilt. It was parked under a huge shady oak tree in their side yard. His girlfriend, Dottie, was watching over his shoulder as he was doing something under the hood. Her yellow Willy's Jeep convertible was parked behind the Model T, and its shade of yellow was a perfect match for her short blonde hair. I remember thinking this scene I was beholding belonged on the cover of Saturday Evening Post. It was America at its simplest and, perhaps, its best. If Norman Rockwell had seen it, he would've painted it. Guaranteed.

Addictive drugs and opioids had not yet poisoned our population, and churches still influenced our behavior. I remember hearing a group of adults accuse another adult of being "hooked" on valium one time, so I shouldn't say there were no drug problems in Marshall. In the name of accuracy, let me say there were very few drug abusers at that time.

Young people treated their elders with respect, even when they didn't deserve it. Students seldom challenged the authority of their teachers, and parents seemed to be focused on raising their children, not being best friends with them. The rules for living somehow seemed more evident then. We were never confused about the rules at our house. My two brothers and I occasionally tested our parents' patience by getting a little lippy and, maybe, showing some signs of defiance. When we did pull on our leashes, Mother usually reacted differently than Daddy did. Mother would give us a look that said, "You've hurt me." Daddy, on the other hand, would give us a look that said, "I'm gonna hurt you." Both looks were effective and usually whipped us right back into line.

When someone refers to the '50s and '60s as "simpler times," I recommend believing them. To illustrate my point, let me remind folks that one of the most exciting times that happened in America each year back then was when the new car models were unveiled. It was fascinating to see what new features the Detroit engineers had added to each model. The introduction of higher horse-powered engines, new colors, fins, slanted tail lights, rear-mounted radio antennas, power steering, blinkers, and all sorts of other innovations made new-car watching most exciting. I remember Nehls Chevrolet, which was in downtown Marshall, used to completely paper over their showroom windows to keep everyone in suspense until unveiling day came. I recall stalking around their windows, trying to find a tear in their paper that would afford me a sneak peek. There wasn't one. About the only other "big" events in Marshall were the county fair, high school sports, school carnivals, and holiday parades.

Geographically speaking, Marshall was in what was referred to as Little Dixie. Marshall and most of East Texas were homes to many cotton plantations and relied on cotton for the bulk of its livelihood. When the Civil War broke out, Marshall and Texas quickly joined the Confederacy. Marshall even became the capital of Missouri during the Civil War. After the War, Marshall became a commerce center because of Jay Gould's railroad's decision to establish its shops and regional facilities there. It largely remained a railroad town until the end of World War II, when advancing railroad technologies began to obviate the need for the Marshall shops. Employment at the shops started dwindling by the late 1960s and was eliminated by the summer of 1981. The loss of the thousands of jobs the shops had provided was tough on Marshall. Fortunately for Marshall and Harrison County, Thiokol Chemical hired 3,500-4,000 locals for well-paying jobs at their plant in nearby Karnack, a plant that manufactured all sorts of military armaments such as missiles, parachute flairs, and rocket fuel. Its employment level rose with our nation's commitment to the Vietnam War.

In 1960, Marshall's population was 23,846. Today, it is a little less than that. Demographically speaking, Marshall is about 40% white and 40% African-American. In the 1950s and '60s, it was more like 60% African-American and 40% white.

So far, I have talked about the near-utopian lifestyle Marshall residents enjoyed when I was a teenager. The picture I painted with words didn't tell the whole story. The truth is, it was near-utopian if you were white. The blacks were not happy with the world in which they were stuck, and their discontent was about to erupt into tradition-jarring actions designed to correct some of the long-endured wrongs they had suffered. As I record my thoughts about the civil rights events that transpired in Marshall during those fragile times, I realize I am walking through a political correctness minefield. I do so nervously.

Two major African-American institutions of higher education were in Marshall at that time, which helped push Marshall to the forefront of the American Civil Rights Movement. Wiley College and Bishop College (Bishop moved to Dallas in 1961) were ranked as two of the eight largest black colleges in the world in the 1950s. Student and professorial leadership from the colleges operating under the umbrella of the National Association for the Advancement of Colored People met in Marshall and planned the entire sit-in strategy to be implemented throughout the

South. They were aided in their planning efforts by native Marshallite, James Farmer. Farmer graduated with honors from Wiley at the age of seventeen and went on to earn his divinity masters from Howard University. The group recruited students from throughout the United States to participate in the protests and sit-ins. Martin Luther King, Jr., visited Marshall in 1960 and made a powerful, action-inspiring speech at Wiley College about their collective rights to protest and sit-in.

A sit-in at the lunch counter of Woolworth's Five and Dime in Marshall on February 1, 1960, followed closely on the heels of the famous sit-in in Greensboro, North Carolina, making it one of the first sit-ins in America. Twenty were arrested at the sit-in and, the next day, a new group of protesters staged sit-ins at three more Marshall lunch counters. More were arrested, and some 350 protesters gathered at the courthouse to sing freedom songs and chant civil rights slogans. A very large assemblage of whites also assembled at the courthouse, and it looked as though a physical confrontation was inevitable.

A couple of my friends and I had just left the Paramount Theater when the protesters gathered at the courthouse. We watched as our downtown began to crackle with tension, and, as we were running to get out of downtown, the pharmacist at Recknagel's Drug Store snatched us off the sidewalk and pulled us into his shop. He then locked his door and let us stand in his window to watch the harrowing events unfold. Law enforcement officials were trying to disperse the crowd with the help of an amped-up bullhorn. The effort failed. When the protesters started to move en masse toward North Washington Street, members of the Marshall Fire Department turned high-pressure water hoses on the demonstrators. The store in which we stood was right on the corner of the street that circled the courthouse and North Washington. We had the best seats in town for the shocking drama that was playing out right in front of our naïve young eyes. The low rumble of the marchers' voices and the sounds of their shoes clicking on the hand-laid brick streets were overpowered by the sounds of screaming, sirens, the big engines of the fire trucks, and the roar of fast-moving water as it rushed down North Washington, carrying protestors in its wake. Today, I find it so ironic that the very bricks over which they marched and were washed were laid, one at a time, by slaves a century before. The water eventually dispersed the protest, but it did not disperse the movement. Marshall had played a key role in the birth of the American Civil Rights Movement.

Even today, I have trouble describing my reaction to seeing so many of the protesters crash into the wall of Recknagel's right below the window in which I stood because of the high-pressure water. The effects of the jets of the high-pressure water on the protestors was devastating. To this day, I am surprised some of the protestors didn't drown or die from the force of the water. The aftermath of that incredible day was a total blur to me. I knew the blacks were seeking new freedoms and rights, but I didn't know enough to have an opinion on their plight. For Southern white people in my age group, accepting the validity of the protests and the cause of the protesters was very complicated. It required us to condemn the actions of our forefathers and reject the social norms we had been taught for many generations by the people we most loved. I can understand when people who were not raised in the South have trouble understanding the internal struggle we had to sort out. However, rather than condemn us, they would be better served by thanking God they were spared from these conflicts. The heavy, heavy scene that had just played out before my eyes and at my feet left no doubt in my mind that I had just witnessed the making of significant history. I was right.

The Civil Rights Movement stayed on America's front burner for many, many years. The courts struck down segregation and most overt forms of discrimination in the 1960s, but tensions between the races remained razor-sharp throughout my school years. I remember when local leaders would crow about the "great" people who had been raised in Marshall; the list included Lady Bird Johnson, football great Y.A. Tittle, and journalist Bill Moyers. Today, Marshallites have proudly added boxer George Foreman and civil rights leader James Farmer to that list of famous sons and daughters. When I visit Marshall today, I see few, if any, Confederate flags flying or draped across the rear windows of pickup trucks. I no longer see the once commonplace bumper stickers that pictured an old rebel in the uniform of the Confederacy running at you while waving his saber in one hand and a Confederate flag in the other with the caption that read, "Hell No, I Ain't Forgettin!" Small victories but victories just the same.

Tony's Shine Parlor was a one-chair shoe shine shop in a three-chair black barber shop. It was located just off Alamo Street, and it was where many of us boys went for a grade A shoe shine before any big date or special event. Tony was a small black man who was always in a good mood. While pleasant, he just went about his business without a lot of chit-chat. We all assumed he was "just" a shine boy until one day in 1961, an article came out in the Marshall News Messenger about the leaders of the black community. To our great surprise, Tony was listed as the third most influential black leader in Marshall. He was also president of the Marshall chapter of the National Association for the Advancement of Colored People (the NAACP). After learning of his active role in the Civil Rights Movement, most of us kept going to Tony's for our shines, but we tipped better than before.

Soon after the protests I described above, the Civil Rights Movement went national and appeared to put Marshall on the back burner. The professors at Bishop and Wiley who helped organize the protests were fired, and the presidents of the two colleges called for the cessation of "civil disobedience." For whatever reasons – perhaps fear – the vast majority of blacks living in Marshall condemned the protests and made their opposition to further such incidents well-known. All downtown lunch counters were taken out to eliminate sit-ins. Our municipal swimming pool closed to avoid having to allow minorities admittance. Civil rights dominated the national scene, but Marshall went quiet. Black anger simmered below the surface, and whites essentially resumed their pre-confrontation lives. There were hot-heads who were white and hot-heads who were black. These two groups fueled many isolated physical confrontations and were equally blame-worthy. Subtle changes began to take place. Sears took down its signs that specified certain water fountains for "Colored." Public restrooms also changed their signs. Positions began to soften, and moments of two-sided tolerance crept into existence. Change was happening, slower than some desired and faster than others wanted.

I think the 1950s and 1960s were Marshall's glory days. It excelled in economics and education, and it grudgingly faced up to its problems. Today, when I return to Marshall, I see her as a classy lady a little past her prime. There's gray in her hair, and wrinkles on her face, but there's a foundation of beauty and character that will long outlive her admirers and her detractors.

I don't want anyone to feel as though Marshall was Shangri-La, nor do I want anyone to think my hometown was a battlefield. It was neither of those places, and it was both of those places. In general, it was whatever an individual wanted it to be. My dad always told me, "You will find what you are looking for." In Marshall, I found a nourishing community that treated me fairly. It rewarded me when I deserved it and spanked me when I got out of line. I got a fair shake.

Chapter 02

The First Day of Junior High
or, Unbridled Confusion

The year was 1958. It was our first day at Marshall, Texas, Junior High School. My best friend, Terry Weeks, and I hopped out of his mom's big Buick and walked up the soaring front steps of the stately three-story red brick building. We were filled with both excitement and abject fear. Our belief that our ascension to junior high somehow signaled to the world we were more important now than we had been as elementary school "children" caused us to puff out our scrawny chests as though proclaiming our arrival. Also, the mere change of venue to this cavernous institution of "higher education" further fueled our excitement – and our trepidation. This big education edifice was both intimidating and inspiring when compared to our puny South Marshall Elementary School. Though we masked our fears and apprehensions behind the toughest faces we could muster, we knew our stony facades were fragile and were always on the verge of collapsing into shaking and crying for our mothers. Truth be known, Terry and I were probably both on the edge of diarrhea.

As we entered the wide halls of MJHS, we were instantly sucked into the frantic mass of wide-eyed kids who shared a lack of knowledge about where to go and what we were to do if we ever got there. The atmosphere in the giant building seemed to throb with electrically-charged emotions. We seventh-graders were easy to spot. We were the kids with the enlarged eyes, the kids who looked like we would bolt for the exits if anyone said "boo" to us. Terry and I, fearing separation, were darn near hugging as we nudged our way to nowhere. I kept a close eye on Terry because I noticed his eyelids had started rapidly fluttering. I knew from having grown up with Terry that this rapid eye blinking movement signaled Terry's nervousness, if not borderline panic.

Our aimless wanderings ended when we heard an adult's loud, no non-sense voice instructing all seventh-graders to report to the auditorium. The man giving us that order was a huge man named Mr. Ross, a science teacher, whose head was the largest head I had ever seen. I still haven't seen one as large as his. Mammoth. Years before, students had dubbed Mr. Ross "Bear." It fit. Early in the seventh-grade, Phil Parker called Mr. Ross "Bear" to his face. Mr. Ross didn't take kindly to it and chased Phil down two flights of stairs, kicking him in the butt every other step. He was touchy about that nickname.

The moving tide of students swept us right into the huge auditorium, where we grabbed seats near the front and instantly began scanning the crowd in search of friends and fellow Southsiders. My comfort level began to rise as I spotted Charlie Starke, Clarence Warnstaff, Joan Bergstrom, and Ruth Ann McClaran three rows behind us. Tuck Kemper and my girlfriend, Carol Marshall, were behind them. I never got around to asking Tuck what he was doing with "my" Carol. I then found Frank Timmins, Sally Van Wert, Susie Musser, Winston Trench, Lana Faye Hardy, and Nancy Brown toward the back of the auditorium. David Wist and David Applebaum spotted me and started waving their hands to let me know where they were. Shirley McCain was sitting with them. I saw Peggy Daniels and Susan Elliott giggling, which they always did when together. Next, I noticed Kay Wilson and Beverly Archer looking all serious and posed with pens in hand, ready and eager to take copious notes as I expected they would be. Lastly, I spotted Richard Magrill and Don Pope sneaking into the back of the auditorium just before a hush crept over the fidgety kids. By the time our new principal, Miss Emma Mae Brotze, called us to order, Terry and I had spotted most of our buds. Their presence added immensely to our growing comfort.

Miss Brotze was a tall, erect, white-haired lady with a deep voice that was confident and firm. Her eye contact was debilitating and had the ability to nail you to the back of your seat. Her mere presence seemed to fill the auditorium, and she quickly reigned in the wiggling, giggling, yakking seventh-graders. As she stared out across the sea of kids, I quickly thought of what a great prison warden she could have been. I now realize the two jobs had more in common than I knew at that time. Believe me, if she had walked into a Pentagon meeting of generals, she would have owned the room. As we entered the auditorium, we were handed a booklet entitled

"PRESENTING Marshall Junior High School." Its first page simply stated, "WELCOME! LET'S GET ACQUAINTED WITH JUNIOR HIGH." After a couple of welcome letters, quite a bit about the history of Marshall's public education, a list of teachers, and a recitation of some of the rules, there was a page devoted to our school prayer and school song. After her welcome and a handful of introductions, Miss Brotze had those of us who had served as presidents of our elementary school student councils say a few words. Scintillating, I'm sure. Then we were all given paperwork to fill out. It asked the standard questions, such as name, address, phone number, etc. As we were filling it out, Terry leaned into me, and we double-checked to make certain he had spelled his first name, Opha, correctly. He had. Next, we were informed of our homeroom numbers and our homeroom teachers' names. We were then sent off to find them. My homeroom teacher was Miss Lucille Estelle, who happened to live next door to my longtime friend Sally Van Wert. The room number was 221. Terry was sent another direction to Mrs. Williamson's homeroom, but before parting, we picked a spot at which to meet when we broke for lunch. I knew quite a few of my homeroom classmates, either from South Marshall, from church, or from having played sports with or against them. I instantly liked Miss Estelle and went home that day thinking everything was going to be just fine. So did Terry, and his rapid eye blinking had ceased.

Well, there you have it. We were in junior high, and a whole new way of living had just swallowed us up.

Chapter 03

A Comb, a Butt Kicking, and Communal Showers

The first week or so of the seventh-grade was a bit of a challenge, to say the least. The entire routine was more complicated than it had been in elementary school. Different classrooms for each subject spread out in the biggest building most of us had ever set foot in, different teachers for each subject, having no recess, the ability to leave the campus for lunch, meeting a whole bunch of new folks, and finding out where we fit in in the new pecking order kept us in a cloud of confusion for a while. Semi-lost kids wandering around the cavernous hallways were the rule, not the exception.

In the sixth grade, Miss Badget taught all my subjects except music. Miss Preston taught my music class (at least, she did when she could stay awake). Once, when Miss Preston asked for volunteers to play in a start-up South Marshall Elementary School Band, I volunteered. My music career never got off the ground because she told me I had no musical talent and that there was no place in the band for me. Every day after that rejection, I bugged Miss Preston about being in the band. Finally, in obvious frustration, she relented and told me I could play the comb in the band. For the musically-challenged among you, let me enlighten you as to how one plays the comb. Simply wrap a piece of toilet tissue around your pocket comb, hold it to your lips, and hum into it. The resultant sound is supposed to be akin to the sound made by plucking a Jew's harp – whatever that is. Impressive, huh?

That night, around the dinner table, I told my family about being selected as the new band's comb player. Everyone, even my always-proper mother, burst out laughing. Despite my humiliation, after supper, I "borrowed" Brother Homer's Ace comb, wrapped it in toilet paper, and sat on the front porch to practice. I hummed, blew, and hummed some more, but I couldn't get any sound out of the Ace. The only thing I got from trying to play the comb was ridicule from my brothers and a smile on my face caused by the tickling of my lips that occurred when I hummed the comb. I resigned from the band the next day. I knew it was okay with Miss Preston because she just nodded and went about her business. Down deep, I knew Miss Preston was right. I had no musical talent.

Perhaps because Miss Preston rejected me for membership in the band and, in essence, eliminated a career in music for me, I will share a little information and gossip about her with you. She struggled mightily to stay awake during class. She would frequently nod off right in the middle of some rousing chorus. Rumor was that Mrs. Preston liked her Jim Beam whiskey and sipped on it between classes. A classmate named Billy said she kept a half-pint of whiskey in her piano bench, under the sheet music for "Goober Peas." Now, Billy was known to frequently stretch the truth, so I cannot verify that Miss Preston was a nipper. Down deep, I suspect Billy may have been right.

For those of you unfamiliar with the old Confederate soldier ditty, "Goober Peas," here's the last verse and chorus:

> *Just before the battle, the General heard a row*
> *He said, "The Yanks are coming, I hear their rifles now"*
> *He turned around in wonder and what do you think he sees?*
> *The Georgia Militia eating goober peas.*
> *(chorus) Peas, peas, peas, peas, eating goober peas*
> *Goodness how delicious, eating goober peas*

This song was a mainstay for our elementary school choir in Marshall, offering a solid hint as to which side East Texas supported in the Civil War. FYI: a goober pea is a peanut.

My final thought on Miss Preston is that she never seemed happy. I always wondered why she seemed so sad. I actually worried about her. She wore a constant frown, one that was punctuated by sad eyes. I now wish I had befriended her and tried to put a smile on her face.

As seventh-graders, we shared the hallways, cafeteria, campus, and restrooms with eighth and ninth-graders. I had never gone to school with people who shaved before. Some looked to me like they were on leave from the Army. I gave them a wide berth in the hallways and, when I had to pee, I chose the urinal that afforded me the most privacy so I wouldn't be put to shame by some big ninth-grader.

The girls were glorious. They were changing, and so was I. It was like God had flipped a switch on the girls during the summer and changed them from kickball-playing girls into make-up-wearing, leg-shaving, sweet-smelling, bra-wearing young women. It was terribly hard to listen in class with these new-found goddesses sprinkled all around me, diverting my attention.

A major, but subtle, challenge that emerged in this new environment came from realizing all these "new" kids had no idea how smart I was, how fast I could run, how tough I was, or how suave I was. Everyone started with a clean slate and had to re-establish his or her creds with their new classmates and teachers.

Honestly, I was shocked at how many of the new kids were very smart and, in fact, were smarter than me. I'm still blown away by how much faster Becky Fitch read than I did in Mrs. Eulyne LaFoy's reading class. Becky must have been exceedingly limber or boneless because when Mrs. LaFoy passed out our reading materials, she would eagerly take them and curl herself into a ball, instantly losing herself in the new reading material. I was so caught up in watching how fast Becky turned her pages and assessing how she could wad herself up like an old piece of Double Bubble, I couldn't get on about my reading. In math, I didn't even belong on the same planet as Bob Power, David Wist, Doc Roberts, Joan Bergstrom, John Tebbetts, and Robert Nader. At South Marshall Elementary, I felt as though I was probably in the top ten of the smartest students. In junior high, I hoped I was in the top ten percent. Honestly, I almost certainly overestimated my brilliance in both cases. Also, it didn't take long for me to realize that some of my new classmates could outrun me, out jump me, and throw a football as far as I could. None of these physical shortcomings bothered me much because I could still hold my own quite nicely in athletics.

Truth be told, I entered junior high thinking I was a pretty tough kid, more than able to take care of myself. I had been involved in skirmishes with kids from all over town and had always faired quite nicely, thank you. Well, that bubble burst for me one day during seventh-grade physical education. We were playing flag football, and a shoving match broke out between Rodney and Davey Lee Bell. In fairly short order, Davey Lee was doing all the shoving, and Rodney became a reluctant shovee. It was clear to all that Rodney wanted to withdraw from this situation, but Davey Lee wouldn't let him off the hook.

In a moment of empathetic stupidity, I stepped between them and told Davey Lee to leave Rodney alone. Davey Lee did leave Rodney alone.

He started shoving me instead. I did a dumb thing. I shoved him back. Lordy, Lordy, it was as though I had let the Tasmanian Devil out of his cage. Before I even realized a fight had broken out, the tough Northsider had butted me in the privates and cold-cocked me with a powerful right to the left side of my head when I bent over in pain from the crotch shot. An old fashioned East Texas ass-kicking was underway, and I was the kickee. He served me a steady diet of eye-crossing head butts below the waist, roundhouse rights, and effective left jabs. I did manage to hit him back quite a few times in the face, but, while his butt-bam-bam program hurt me a lot, my blows to him just seemed to make him angry.

I finally surrendered, totally insecure in the knowledge that some of these new boys were a hell of a lot tougher than yours truly. To amplify my embarrassing loss, I had to wear my defeat for about a week in the form of two black eyes. A rematch was always out of the question. One dance with Davey Lee Bell was enough for this boy. Mr. Bell racked up an impressive number of fisticuff victories that seventh-grade year, including one over my then-friend, Roy Lee Fry, who – like me – had come to junior high thinking he was a tough hombre. I don't know what made Davey Lee Bell so tough. It was like he carried nitroglycerin in his pockets and, if you touched him, it exploded. It took very little provocation to set him off. When he wasn't destroying some kid, he was a slow-talking, slow-walking, nice guy, but take it from me: if you are ever in Davey Lee's company, don't touch him, and just agree with him. He's always closer to exploding than you realize.

My dad was big on me and my two brothers suffering through what he called "learning experiences," figuring they would help prepare us for a life that was very unpredictable and not always on our side. Well, I learned a few things from this particular "learning experience." The next time I see someone in a shoving match with Davey Lee Bell, he's on his own. It's hard to maintain a "tough kid" image in junior high when you have to walk around school with two black eyes sustained from a butt whipping witnessed by forty or so classmates.

You know, some of the transitional adjustments to junior high were pretty simple and easy to pull off. While we wore sneakers in sixth grade, it was loafers in junior high. Tee shirts were out, and collared shirts were a must. That little lifestyle change was really hard on Charlie Starke because he was unabashedly devoted to wearing white tee shirts all the time. Smirking and acting "cool" were more in vogue in junior high. It was normal to never act surprised or impressed – uncool, man. Childlike exuberance or innocence were signs that earned you the label of being "immature," and that was a real no-no for a cool kid. If you read this paragraph and can't relate to anything I said, well, you were probably more comfortable in your skin at age thirteen than I was.

In elementary school, each grade had its own playground area, and we weren't allowed to infringe on another grade's turf. In junior high, everyone, even high schoolers, shared the same grounds. Our playgrounds were now referred to as our campus. In grade school, we weren't allowed to leave the schoolground. In junior high and high school, we were. All these changes meant us newbies had to figure out where to hang out. Most of the girls hung out on the campus. The boys? Not so much. Given a chance to leave the campus was a freedom most boys couldn't resist. As a rule, it's the nature of boys – particularly those of junior high age – to stretch their leashes as far as they can. It's a tendency many boys retain throughout their lives. All that is to say, one of the things a new seventh-grader had to do early on was to claim some real estate where he and his buddies could hang out before school and during lunch time.

There were a lot of hang-out options available such as Andrews Hobby Shop – right across the street from the east side of the campus, it was the perfect spot for model builders, science nerds, model train collectors, etc. It sold candy and sodas but no sandwiches or lunch food. Mr. Andrews was grumpy and wouldn't let non-customers hang out in front of his store, particularly the "thuggy" kids, most of whom smoked. Several of such kids hung out just down the street from the Hobby Shop. They also hung around Abel's Grocery Store – the small, dark, old-timey neighborhood store, the entire stock of which could fit in the trunk of a car – located on a one-way street about a half-block off the campus. Mr. Abel was very old, very bald, and very non-communicative. If he had a personality at all, he must have been saving it because it never showed itself to us kids. He only turned his lights on if someone came into the store. Just thrifty, I suppose, or perhaps he couldn't sleep with the lights on. When pushed, he would make you a baloney sandwich with cheese. Only smokers with long, oily hair combed in duck-tails hung out in front of Abel's. My friend, Henry Croom, who grew up in North Carolina, said the kids of his day referred to that kind of hairdo as a "d.a," or a duck's ass. The Maverick Grill was another hot spot located across the street from the southside of the campus, it was housed in a Quonset hut. It served burgers, fries, and other kinds of sandwiches. It had a bit of a loyal following, but for some reason, it didn't work out for my pals and me; a block or so west of the Maverick Grill was a small white frame building that was either a tiny grocery store or a café. It had no sign, but it always had a leather-jacketed, greasy-haired group of smokers standing around on the bare dirt in front of it. I never mustered the nerve to check it out. The thought of penetrating the gang that hung out there and their ever-present smoke cloud was just too daunting.

It was across the street from our junior high football practice field, and we could generally hear the rowdy cast of characters cussing, laughing, spitting, and yelling over the grunts and sounds of cracking shoulder pads and helmets emanating from our practice. At the end of our practices, the footballers from the 7th, 8th, and 9th grade teams were called together by the coaches for sprints and laps. One day during laps, the crowd from the unnamed hang-out spotted one of their own jogging by and started calling him by name and asking him if he wanted a cigarette. Our player's name was Jesse Jeter, a well-built, able eighth-grader who looked and acted older than his grade would suggest. Jesse was a promising fullback and linebacker. He was easygoing and got along well with everyone, but he was totally irritated and embarrassed by his buds from across the street, and he tried to shut them up by shaking his head and waving both arms in the "stop it" mode. Seeing the distress they were causing their friend only spurred them on, and they got louder and louder. Smoking was a major no-no for athletes, and Jesse definitely didn't want his coaches to hear his taunters offering him smokes. If they heard, they ignored it, perhaps in deference to the talent he appeared to have.

While we were entertained by their antics, these rascals and this joint were not right for our gang. We picked a spot on the street corner just north of the Hobby Shop.

You know, hanging around the older boys and learning our places in the pecking order were important rites of passage as we entered the worlds of junior and senior high schools. The older boys seemed to get a kick out of scaring the younger ones. For a while, it was all the rage for the older/stronger boys to grab a frightened underclassman and stick an opened full bottle of soda down the back of his Levi jeans – upside down, of course. The newly initiated kid had to go through the rest of the day looking like he had peed on himself and enduring the wet, sticky Levis. I don't remember any of these hazings being particularly dangerous or harmful. Well, now that I think of it, I believe taking a boy's pants off and hiding them from him could actually leave some emotional scars, but, thankfully, those events rarely occurred. Some older boys threatened underclassmen with taking their pants off just to plant the possibility in the younger student's mind. It worked and made for some leery kids for a while. In general, these pranks were just part of letting us know we were the low men on the totem pole.

I remember once when some older tough guys encircled me and told me what they were going to do to me. I was scared and about to try to break through their circle for a dash to safety when a tenth grader named Garnet Bell told them to leave me alone, telling them I was a good guy.

Apparently, Garnet's street creds carried some weight and, after he vouched for me, the guys always treated me like I was one of them. Garnet, wherever you are, please accept my belated thank you. Bullying has never been fun or nice, but in the 1950s and 1960s, we had to learn to deal with it on our own. It was, you know, a rite of passage, or what Daddy would call a "learning experience." If my brothers or I ever allowed ourselves to be bullied, we received a frosty reaction from Daddy. He expected us to stand our ground, even it meant getting our butts kicked.

When the lunch bell rang, we had thirty-five minutes to eat and return to class. We usually ran like the dickens to Downtown Marshall, which was about 10-12 long blocks from school, and grabbed a hamburger at the Waffle Shop, Tiny Grill, Fry Hodge Drug Store, or the Coffee Cup Café. Before our last bites hit our stomachs, we were on the street, racing back to school, and trying to beat the bell. On some days, we grabbed a burger at Steven's Burgers and Fries, which was only half a block from campus. Their service was terribly slow, so unless you got in their order line early, you would be late for class. My best bud, Terry, beat this hectic system of run-eat-run. He had study hall in the junior high library for the hour just before lunch. This library allowed students to sign out to go to the high school library for "special" research. Terry would sign out of our junior high library to go to the high school library nearly every day, but he never went. Instead, he added this free hour onto his thirty-five-minute lunch break and enjoyed an extended lunch period. Good thinking, Terry.

One of the new "things" we faced in the seventh-grade was physical education. We were told to bring our tennis shoes (all sneakers were called tennis shoes in Marshall back then), gym shorts, a tee-shirt, and a towel to the gym where we would change into P.E. garb, do physical stuff, shower, dry off, re-dress, and return to class. While it may sound like fairly simple instructions, it proved to be confounding to two of the smartest boys in the seventh-grade. Bobby and Gary apparently missed the part of the instructions that told us our change of clothes was to occur in the gym.

As instructed, they brought their gear to school and put it in their lockers. When the bell rang, signaling it was time for their P.E. class, they went to their lockers, undressed down to their underwear, and put on their gym clothes. The hallway was full of classmates going from one class to the next, but it didn't stop the two brainiacs from doing their near-full montes right in front of everyone. There was some laughing and pointing that went on, but, you know, I'd bet there were quite a few other seventh-grade boys who saw what was happening and wondered if they should change into their gym clothes in front of their lockers. No one was locked into the junior high routine yet, and uncertainty was the order of the day.

The concept of showering together after P.E. was new to all of us and caused quite a bit of consternation to some. The boys who had some pubic hair showed it off during shower time, while late bloomers tried to get an end shower nozzle where they could turn their backs to the masses and avoid showcasing their immaturity. When drying off, if you noticed someone trying to check your privates, the practice was to use a towel to hide that area of your body and act as though you were just drying off, thus blocking the nosy classmate's visual inspection. Some of us may have returned to class with damp bodies and wet between the toes, but our privates were totally dry. I don't know for sure, but I suspect that girls suffered similar anxieties regarding development.

Sometimes, shower-generated rumors spread. It was the consensus that a boy named Phil had the most pubic hair, elevating his ranking in the new order of things. On the downside, another boy, who shall remain nameless, was rumored to have an el-shaped penis. No one ever asked him to go through an inspection, but the mere possibility that he had an oddly shaped penis slotted him rather low on the pecking (or should I say "pecker") order.

I had gone through elementary school feeling rather confident and totally unthreatened. Most of that bravado fell away as I took in my new environs and the new boys with whom I was sharing it. As I said before, I was struck by how many of these guys shaved, how many had "real" muscles, and by how many of them were a heck of a lot closer to manhood than I was. I knew many of these boys had failed a year or two and were older than I was, but I found very little solace in those facts. They were now my peers.

I know profiling is no longer politically correct or acceptable, but I gotta tell you, you needed to be able to profile these new folks at junior high, or you could have ended up in a whole bunch of trouble. There had been no thugs at South Marshall Elementary School. There were some at Marshall Junior High School. Thugs – and we did call them thugs back then – seemed to hang together and share a number of common characteristics. They seldom smiled or laughed, unless it was more of a smirk than a smile, or their laugh was derisive versus happy. They usually looked either sad or angry. I think these frowns and scornful stares were part of a façade they were trying to project to imply their toughness. It worked. The other possibility was that they really were sad or angry – or both. Unfortunately, many of them did, in fact, come from tough home environments. They mostly dressed alike, combed their hair alike, and talked about the same things: sex, knives, motorcycles, combs, and fighting. I am ill-equipped to analyze the make-up of a thug, but I, along with my other classmates, had no trouble identifying one when we saw one. They seemed to relish their images as tough guys.

I had played a lot of baseball with boys who went the "tough guy" route when they hit junior high. We had been friends during the summers and had often slept over at each other's homes. These friendships and our mutual respect didn't stop when we got to junior high. They served me well in that I was welcomed into their "inner circles" and allowed to move freely back into my own world with no trouble or ridicule. The freedom to hang with whomever I chose was quite instructive. It taught me these "toughs" were often from loving families and were very nice kids. The barriers that separated them from other kids were usually economic or perhaps the feeling that life had dealt them a losing hand. As I stated before, we had to be able to profile to avoid unwanted trouble. However, in doing so, I am certain some very nice folks got wrongly labeled along the way.

Suffice it to say, as time passed, we all seemed to settle into our new lives as seventh-graders, eighth-graders, and ninth-graders. We found comfort in our routines, learned how to read our teachers, got involved with school activities, and made lots of new friends. Life would have been simple and almost predictable if the monster of puberty hadn't descended on us and worked us over. In retrospect, I think a very fine line separates puberty and insanity.

Chapter 04

Puberty:
Guilt, Frustration, Passion, Insanity, Etc.

There have been several books written incorporating the phrase "The Age of Guilt" in its title. I've never read any of them, nor do I have the foggiest idea about any of the subjects with which they dealt. However, if I ever write a book entitled "The Age of Guilt," it will be about the early years of puberty.

When I thought about writing this book about my junior high and high school experiences in the 1950s and 1960s, I was keen not to make it just about the arrival of puberty and the resultant chaos. Lots of other authors had amply covered that subject. While I worked hard to not turn this book into a treatise on puberty, it would be disingenuous of me to downplay the magnitude of the impact puberty had on my – and most everyone else's – teen years. The confusion that sprang from puberty caused a major re-wiring in the brains of us boys and, maybe, some girls. So, hang on.

I was raised in the First Baptist Church of Marshall, Texas, and I loved it and the folks with whom I worshipped. My great Sunday School teachers like Mrs. Rountree, Mrs. Fowler, Mrs. Hill, Mr. Graham, Mr. Scott, and Mr. Thompson were important positive influences in my life. Nevertheless, part of being a Baptist was feeling guilty. It was a part of our dogma. If you couldn't think of anything to feel guilty about, well, you should feel guilty about not being able to think of anything to feel guilty about. Know what I mean? When I walked into my Baptist church, I felt guilty before I sat down. I sometimes felt like I should just enter and surrender to Satan, the sheriff, or the preacher. I had been word-whipped into believing I was beyond redemption. If I felt like that before I reached puberty, imagine how I felt after this alien took control of my mind and my body. Have you ever tried to shrink out of sight in a Baptist pew? It can't be done.

I grew up listening to some wonderfully gifted preachers. Most of their messages were ones of hope and eternal bliss, but, perhaps unwittingly, they often put so many doctrinal obstacles between flock members and Heaven that achieving a happy ending seemed impossible. Where was the hope when they spent two or three sermons on the evils associated with the way Elvis Presley swiveled his hips on the Ed Sullivan Show? If these leaders of men preached against dancing, co-ed hayrides, and having co-ed Sunday School classes, what would they think if they knew what I was thinking about most of my waking hours? I thought – or at least wondered – about sex, even in church. Like it or not, God had made some major improvements in the appearance of girls, and I noticed. When I should have been listening to Reverend Rutledge describe Jesus turning water into wine at the wedding reception, I was imagining all the girls in the third pew naked. Clearly, I suffered from "Pew Passion," a condition for which there was no vaccine. By the way, I don't do that nearly as much today as I did back then.

I rocked along through the seventh-grade content to just admire girls. It was obvious the girls of summer had become the young women of autumn. I didn't even know enough about sex, the female anatomy or the mechanics of sex stuff to have good fantasies. My fantasies lacked enough details to be fun. While I imagined sex and dreamed of it, if it had come to me on a silver platter, it would have had to come with a how-to manual.

A foundation stone in my sexual advancement was laid one night in room #30 at the Bob Hope Motel in Marshall. Relax. It's not what you are thinking. You see, the Bob Hope Motel was owned by Mrs. Robert Hope. She was my good friend David Wist's grandmother, and we all called her "Neenie." David and his older brother, Bobby, also a good friend of mine, often spent weekends at the motel. On this particular night, Neenie let David and me stay in #30, a real thrill to two thirteen-year-old boys. When we settled into our room, David looked at me like he had just swallowed the proverbial canary and pulled a book out of his overnight bag. It was a copy of D.H. Lawrence's, *Lady Chatterley's Lover*, the controversial novel that had been banned by all school libraries and most public libraries in the United States because of its explicit descriptions of Mrs. Chatterley's sexual re-awakening in the arms of her gardener. David had found the book in Neenie's library. One could have heard a pin drop as David and I took turns reading the "juicy" parts out loud. We read until our pounding hearts could take no more. We then just laid back onto our pillows and stared at the ceiling until sleep crept up on us. We were shocked, over-stimulated, and both of us felt like we had just been in the devil's bedroom. This session had to have been one of those "learning experiences" Daddy told me would visit themselves upon me.

Then, in the eighth-grade, things started to change. I quit longing for Annette Funicello and the other cute Mouseketeers and started lusting for Sandra Dee. I was shocked to learn of the marked differences between thinking a girl was pretty and outright lusting for her. It was a jump-back moment. I started preening in front of the mirror, hoping my looks would win me admiring looks from girls. It was a longshot, but I hoped.

My longtime friend, Lynn Abney, had a pool party at her house for about eight of us, four girls and four boys. I guess it was the first time I had paid attention to how these girls with whom I was growing up had blossomed into well-shaped, tantalizing young women. They were stunning in swimsuits, and I probably did a lousy job of hiding my gawking. They were all pretty, but I couldn't take my eyes off Lynn. Oh, my. We all played, giggled, and teasingly brushed up next to each other until it was almost time to go home. As we all climbed out of the pool and started to dry off, Lynn and I somehow ended up over behind some camellia bushes where she kissed me. Not a peck, a kiss. A French kiss that made my knees buckle. I didn't even know what a French kiss was and, at first, I thought Lynn had a loose screw to want to do that to me. I quickly recovered and enjoyed that kiss all the way to my toes. After that kiss, I left for home, but I left knowing my life had been changed forever. I now had material for a good fantasy. That was some kiss.

The eighth and ninth-grade years were years of gradual progress. Sexually, I was stuck somewhere between "want to" and "can't do." My body and mind were telling me to go for it, but my heart and church-instilled guilt took root on my shoulder. Another problem I faced was where to go if, in fact, I did go for it.

In Walt Disney's movie, "Pinocchio," Jiminy Cricket became Pinocchio's conscience, always perched on his shoulder and whispering in the young boy's ear. Once, he told the wooden boy, "Yep, temptations. They're the wrong things that seem right at the time, but, uh… even though the right things may seem wrong sometimes, sometimes the wrong things may be right at the wrong time, or vice versa. Understand"? Pinocchio didn't have a clue as to what Jiminy had told him, and I was equally confused by the ever-present clash between desire and Baptist theology.

My friend, Jean Decker, who grew up in Missouri, told me her mother told her lightning was God taking a picture. She added that in high school she was leery of dating during a thunderstorm and would not go parking if there was even one dark cloud in the sky. She wanted no record of her activities. That was guilt at war with passion.

Late one afternoon, Terry and I were sitting on his front porch, just killing time by watching a new family move into the house next door to his. We noticed they had a daughter who looked to be about our age, so we ambled over to their yard to say hello. Her name was Jeanie, who turned out to be two years older than us. She was in the tenth grade, two grades ahead of us. She came over to Terry's to listen to records and get acquainted. A pretty girl, she also had a terrific personality, and the three of us hit it off immediately. I'm not certain how long it took or how it got started, but Jeanie started handing out kisses to Terry and me, alternatingly, of course. This smooch-a-thon went on for some time and may have led to more shenanigans had not Mrs. Youngblood come to take Jeanie home for dinner. There was never a follow-up session to that delightful evening, but the three of us formed very close friendships, friendships that lasted well beyond high school and college. That night, Jeannie not only moved into a new house, she helped move two love rookies a little farther along the road to sexual progress. It was just another learning experience for us.

I had "dated" Carol Marshall through all of the sixth grade and half of the seventh-grade, and when she dumped me for Wist, I played the field until a super-cute little Italian girl named Susan Cacioppo, who had just moved to Marshall, caught my eye. After a proper courtship, we agreed to go steady with each other. We did so until we called it quits some time during the eighth-grade. Susan and her family moved to St. Louis at the end of the ninth-grade. I remember the last time I saw Susan. She was cleaning out her locker, and she was wearing a white blouse and a very dark skirt. Even though we weren't an item at the time, it was a sad day for me. Both Carol and Susan were wonderful girls, and I am glad they were in my life before lust started driving my bus.

There are a lot of things I can't tell you about my ninth-grade puberty-related activities, and even fewer about my high school years, but there are a couple I will share. First of all, my girlfriend in the ninth- grade was the pretty, popular, and delightful, Diane Whitis. Diane was a cheerleader, and I was on the football team. I had sustained some broken ribs in a game and had to sit out several games while healing. Diane's mother usually drove her to out-of-town games in their green Plymouth, and one time I eschewed riding the team bus to Tyler in favor of riding with Diane and her mother. Diane's mother and little brother, Mickey, rode in the front; Diane and I sat in the back. Since the nighttime darkness afforded us privacy, Diane and I sat as close to each other as possible and just looked mushily at each other, grinning like Cheshire cats the entire time.

When I worked up my nerve to put my arm around her, I accidently brushed her right breast, or what I thought was her right breast. Truthfully, I didn't feel a thing. At our 50th high school reunion, I asked Diane if she remembered me brushing her boob. She remembered our cuddle-filled ride to Tyler but recalled nothing else. She just laughed and told me she didn't have any boobs in the ninth-grade. Back then, the size of her boobs, or lack thereof, didn't matter to me. The incident went down in my mind as the first time I had ever touched a female's bosom.

Right here is about as good of a place as any to mention our junior high cheerleaders. It was a big deal to be a cheerleader, and we had some real cute girls patrolling our sidelines. Diane was joined by Marteal Mullikin, Amanda Stallcup, Susie Musser, Martha Scott, and Dale York. There was something about cheerleader costumes that turned cute girls into gorgeous girls. To date a cheerleader back then was to walk in high cotton.

Junior High Cheerleaders (l to r): Susie Musser, Amanda Stallcup, Diane Whitis, Martha Scott, Dale York

Puberty Drove the Car

The advancement of my puberty-inspired longings received a big boost when Mother and Daddy let me start driving our old 1950 Chevrolet to school. Since both parents worked, it was practical for me to have a car in which to get around. I started driving to school months before I got my driver's license. In fact, when I was doing my student driving in the Driver's Education class, my instructor, Coach Wooten, would often comment on how well I had or had not parked my Chevy that day as we passed it going to or returning from my driving lesson. Having a car in which to scoot around Marshall significantly advanced the number of opportunities I had for cuddling and kissing. Nothing dramatic or earth-shaking happened in that old Chevy, but enough did happen in it to make me glad cars couldn't talk. Thank you, General Motors, for nudging me along the road to fantasy fulfillment.

At about this time in our lives, Terry and I decided we needed to buy some condoms. We just knew we were ever-so-close to losing our virginity, so we needed to be ready when that break-through moment came. I was elected to go into the drug store and make the purchase because I was taller than Terry. Back then, condoms weren't on public display. They were kept under the counter in the pharmacy, meaning their purchase required a face-to-face encounter with an adult – an adult who probably knew you and your family. By the way, at the ripe old age of 14, I didn't know what a condom was. I had only heard those thing-a-mabobs called "rubbers."

Finally, after a taxing bout with runaway anxiety and waiting for the counter area to clear, I sidled up to the counter. The pleasant pharmacist asked how he could help me. I tried to deepen my voice to appear older, but when I told him I needed some rubbers, my fear had raised my voice to a pitch high enough to break crystal. I had wanted to sound, act, and look like Robert Mitchum, but I sounded like Tweety Bird, acted like Goofy, and looked like Barney Fyffe. Despite the embarrassing displays of my youth and insecurities, he asked me what kind I wanted. I had found some in Daddy's dresser drawer one time that looked like gold coins, so I asked him for the ones that looked like gold coins. Clever, huh? To my surprise – and great relief – he pulled a three-pack out from under the counter. I paid him, took the paper bag, and darn near ran for the front door. No one ever told me the road to manhood had so many potholes in it.

When Terry and I got home, we locked ourselves in his bedroom and opened one of the "gold coins" to study it and figure out how to use it.

We read the instructions, committed them to memory, and each secreted a rubber into our billfold. Neither of us had the foggiest idea about how long it would be before either of those prophylactics would be called into service. After an extended period of time, I noticed my round gold coin was imprinting itself on the outside of my billfold, so I blew it up like a balloon and tied it to a rural mailbox. I think Terry carried his until it disintegrated.

Before I leave this discourse on condoms, I must tell you about an incident that may have had ripple effects far beyond our wildest imaginings. My friend, Paul, was working one summer as the night attendant at a local Humble (now Exxon) gas service station. It was another slow night in Marshall, so several of us interrupted our Grand Avenue cruising to stop in and visit with Paul. It was obviously a slow night at the Humble station, too, because we found Paul sitting in the office with a large pile of Trojan condoms strewn around on the desk in front of him. We asked him what he was doing, and he told us he was poking holes in all the rubbers with a straight pin. It's amazing what boredom will cause a fellow to do. Guess what? Mike bought two of the punctured Trojans from Paul. Really, Mike?

There are more stories about boy-girl interactions in other parts of this book, but I have a few closing thoughts about learning to cope with puberty with which to end this chapter.

Just think of the power of puberty. Once it arrives, it stays with us the rest of our lives. In the beginning, it basically arms puppy love and can make it potent. It's powerful enough to cause hair to grow, pimples to mar our childish looks, our voices to deepen, and instant erections to pop up. It can cause fist fights, inspire dreams, and make us do stupid things. It can create internal wars involving right versus wrong. It can cause the sealing of a relationship, or it can cause the destruction of a relationship. There is one seldom-discussed positive thing that comes from puberty. Almost overnight, a boy lit-up by puberty is able to drift into sexual fantasies that are incredibly creative and imaginative. His imagination is honed to a fine edge and can take him into places and put him into situations his pre-pubescent brain couldn't have come up with in a million years. Imagination and creativity are good things to possess. Right? Ultimately, puberty in action can lead to babies being born, wanted or unwanted. We experience very few things in life that are more powerful than puberty, and it comes to us at such a young age. How we handle it often defines us as individuals throughout our lives.

Chapter 05

The Spotlight on Big Time Junior High Sports

In elementary school, all our sports were played on the schoolground. We had no uniforms, no coaches, no umpires or referees. The length of recesses determined the length of our games. We chose-up sides each play period, so team make-up changed twice a day. Nobody watched us play, not even the girls. Anytime I made a touchdown or hit a homerun, I looked around to see if Carol, Lynn, Susie, or Dolly noticed. They never did. We made up the rules to fit the size of our teams and our field of play. When we played football, Terry Weeks and Richard Magrill were the best blockers. Gary Sims, Charlie Starke, and John Mark Phillips were the best receivers, while Frank Timmins, Tuck Kemper, and I shared quarterbacking duties. Everyone who wanted to play did play. When football was out of season, we played kickball, softball, or basketball. When we got to junior high, things changed.

In junior high, sports – which were only for boys – took on a more serious, rule-bound face. Many boys moved on from sports, focusing instead on things like academics, band, choir, drama, etc. Those of us who wanted to continue our sports "careers" had to try out for teams, give up our freedoms to coaches, and stay after school for practices. If we made a team, we were outfitted with uniforms but still had to buy the appropriate kinds of shoes. All sneakers were called tennis shoes or "tennies" if we were in cool-talk-mode.

Our first sports season was football. Seventh-graders were on a team called the Midgets. We practiced a lot but had no games. Technically, we were the "C" team for the Mighty Mites, our junior high varsity, which was made up primarily of ninth-graders. I remember absolutely nothing about seventh-grade football because there was absolutely nothing to remember. I take that back. I remember watching our Mighty Mite varsity practice one day, and I saw Paul Ray standing on the sideline with his helmet off. I could not stop staring at him. He was our star fullback and middle linebacker, but what captured my attention was the vast physical difference between him and me. I was normal. Paul Ray was a hugely muscled-up physical specimen that belonged on the Green Bay Packers, not on our junior high Mighty Mites. The term "early maturer" was surely invented to cover Paul Ray's rapid ascension to manhood. He not only shaved, he had a heavy black beard that had to have required two shaves a day. His arms and legs were covered with dark, thick, curly hair, and he was beginning to have a receding hairline. I thanked God right then I didn't have to try to tackle Paul Ray. I also thanked the Lord Paul Ray was nice to all people and didn't eat seventh-graders for lunch. Lastly, we were so low on the totem pole of importance, many aspiring stars-in-waiting had to supply their own pads, jerseys, pants, etc. for seventh-grade football. Our school simply didn't have enough equipment to fully outfit everyone so only the most promising athletes got their gear from the school.

Part of the gear we were told to buy was a jockstrap. It was required to protect our genitalia from injury. Most of us knew virtually nothing about jockstraps – or our genitalia, for that matter – but it made us feel very manly to tell the clerk at Logan and Whaley Sporting Goods we needed a jockstrap. The size of the jockstrap was printed on the front of the strap itself, enabling all your teammates to see what size you wore as you were putting on or taking off your practice uniforms. The Logan and Whaley salesman gave most all of us smalls, much to our collective chagrin. We were hoping for larges because we thought the size was based on how big your privates were. We later learned, with great relief, that the size of a jockstrap had nothing to do with how large or small our genitals were but, in fact, only related to our waist sizes. As Daddy would have said, I had just had a learning experience.

Eighth-grade football was a step up to the Mighty Mite "B" team. This team was dubbed the Termites by head coach McNatt. We were outfitted in old, worn-out gear and uniforms surplused several years earlier. My stuff was in pretty good shape, but that was not the case for Vernard Grimes. Vernard was a seventh-grader who was skilled enough to make the Termites but not skilled enough to get a decent uniform or equipment. When it came time for him to get a helmet, the only one left was an old Knute Rockne-styled leather one that fit his head like a glove. It couldn't have prevented a bee sting, much less a bit of brain-jarring contact. When Vernard tugged it on, the top of it formed a point that made it look like the seventh-grader was wearing half of a large pecan shell. That helmet had to have been mildewing in an abandoned equipment locker since the 1930s. We called Vernard "Pecan" throughout the season.

D. H. Martin, Paul Wood, and Palmer Pratt were talented enough players as eighth-graders to make the varsity Mighty Mites. I did well enough to make the Mighty Mites for three or four games that year. I seldom played when I was "called up," but one time, we were well ahead of Carthage and were about to score again, when Coach McNatt sent me in to replace Bob Bibb at left halfback. I was scared to death but, as fate would have it, our quarterback, Deacon Lewis, called 23-left. That meant he was going to hand the ball off to me for a quick hitter up the middle. Not knowing exactly where to run, I took the hand-off and simply grabbed the jersey of Jimmy, our left tackle, and let him pull me into the end zone for a touchdown. Everyone made me feel incredibly good by patting me on the back and congratulating me. The praise should have gone to Jimmy, but I totally ate it up.

It was the tradition that after a Mighty Mite football game, all the students gathered at the Corral Club, our teen center, for dancing, ping pong, pool, snacks, socializing, or just standing around looking cool. Because the football players had to shower and change clothes after the game, they were usually the last to arrive. As team members trickled in, all the girls screamed and clapped in greeting the heroes of the night. The night I scored my touchdown in Jimmy's wake, I rode to the Corral with Jimbo Hughes, Butch Kennedy, and Ronnie McMullen. All three were ninth-graders and very good ballplayers. By being able to walk into the Corral Club with the three of them, I felt like I was a real celebrity. On cue, all the girls squealed and clapped and gave us hugs. What a night! It was heady stuff. I remember slow-dancing the night away to the mellow sounds of Tommy Edwards and Johnny Mathis. Thank you, Jimbo, Butch, and Ronnie for enabling me to feel like a big shot that night by letting me ride on your coattails at the Corral Club. Also, thank you, Jimmy, for giving me a special night by pulling me into the end zone for a touchdown.

After those few games I played with the varsity, I finished the season on the Termites. It was where I belonged, plus most of my closest friends were also on the Termites. Weeks, Wist, John Bogue, Phil Parker and Mike Briggs were starters on the line, and all were close friends of mine. Our starting backfield was Roy Lee Fry at quarterback, Mickey

McCay at right halfback, me at left halfback, and I can't remember who started at fullback – maybe Mike Hazelip. It didn't matter because the Termites only played one game.

When football started our ninth-grade year, we were excited. It was our turn to be the hot shot football stars. It was we who would get those nice white and green uniforms and the state-of-the-art pads and helmets. Before our first practice, Head CoachMcNatt gathered us together in the dressing room to lay down the rules we were to follow, what he expected from us in school regarding grades and conduct, and what our practice and game schedules were. We all listened intently as McNatt laid down the law about no smoking, no drinking, eating a good diet, and getting lots of rest. He then told us – rather sheepishly – that we should refrain from masturbating. He went on by telling us that too much masturbation sapped out strength, could cause eye problems, and, ultimately, blindness if it went on unchecked. We had all heard a rumor about this blindness thing, so we figured that if our coach said it was true, it had to be so. The minute those words were out of the coach's mouth, one boy started blinking uncontrollably and turned white as a sheet. Obviously, the coach's words about masturbation had hit home with this boy. He might as well had hung a big sign on his chest that said, "GUILTY OF OVER-SELF-STIMULATION." His incessant blinking went on for some time before a group of us assured him he wasn't going blind.

Football in Texas was serious stuff. Junior high coaches coached like they were preparing for the Super Bowl, although the Super Bowl hadn't yet been invented when I was in junior high. Practices were long, hard, and dry. We weren't allowed to drink water or sit down during practice, as it was commonly believed by Marshall coaches at that time that giving a dehydrated kid a sip of water or allowing a bone-weary, and perhaps injured, kid to sit down for a spell would make him "soft." These days, that philosophy sounds as stupid as it actually was. I illustrate the football mindset with this story about our little linebacker, Mike Briggs.

Mike was small in stature but muscled up from weight training. He was also a tough kid who backed off from nothing and no one. At one practice, Mike clanged heads with someone and bit a big chunk of his tongue completely off. He found his tongue in the dirt and held on to it as he continued to play. Blood was pouring out of Mike's mouth and soon had turned the front of his white practice jersey bright red. Seeing this bloody horror caused Coach McNatt to stop practice. When Coach asked Mike what happened, the kid opened his mouth and waggled his half tongue. He then revealed the dirty part of the tongue he was holding. When McNatt finally made sense of what had happened, he had an assistant coach rush Mike and his severed tongue to the hospital. Believe it or not, they successfully sewed Mike's tongue back where it belonged, and he healed just fine. The point to this story is to illustrate the lengths footballers would go to keep from looking like sissies to their coaches and his teammates. As I said, football was serious business in the 1950s-60s. It probably still is.

Our team lost its first two games, but I did well. I ran kick-offs back, ran inside and outside, threw and received passes, and played outside linebacker on defense. However, late in the second game, I was crushed by a defensive end and broke all the ribs on my left side, actually separating two of them from my spine and leaving them close to puncturing my lung. This injury put my body on the shelf for most of the remaining season and my mind on injured reserve forever. I was ably replaced by Tuck and Teddie Lee until my late-season return. In my absence, the Mighty Mites went on a tear, starting with a win over Tyler, spurred by Bogue's touchdown reception of a Pratt pass.

My first game back after my injury was against Lufkin, the team with which we were tied for the district lead. There was much build-up about this big game the week before. The coaches named me a captain for this game since I was back in the starting lineup. I even spoke at our huge pep rally. I had heard how Lufkin had obliterated the other teams in our district and about how great their stars, Rocky Thompson and David Brevell were. I was stoked when the game began, and I stayed that way until I got slobberknockered a few times by their big, strong, speedy defense. After four or five of those bone-jarring gang tackles, I realized the fear of re-injuring myself and an innate fear of dying young had conquered my once confident bravado. That's when I decided baseball and basketball were my sports. This captain didn't want the ball anymore. The game stayed close the first four or five minutes. After that, it became painfully evident that Lufkin was a vastly better team than we were. We also discovered that Thompson and Brevell were as good as advertised. Our coach benched me the second half and inserted Teddie Lee at left halfback. Teddie Lee turned out to be the only back we had who could run the ball well against Lufkin. Our hardest game of the season turned out to be his best game of the season. It hurt to realize and admit to ourselves we were the second-best team in our district.

After all was said and done, I loved playing football in junior high. Three of my teammates went on to big universities on football scholarships after starring in high school. They were: quarterback Palmer Pratt (University of Houston), linebacker Roy Lee Fry (Texas A&M), and tackle D. H. Martin (University of Texas). D. H. lettered three years at Texas and earned all-conference honors.

When football season faded away, basketball season was waiting to take over. We had a seventh-grade team, but I'm not certain it had a name. We practiced hard every day in the sweltering girl's gym under the tutelage of Coach Martin. Coach Martin was a somber man whose coaching specialty had been track and field. He was past retirement age and, bless his heart, looked like he had borrowed wrinkles from the future and spread them all over his face. He was kind and encouraging, but basketball wasn't really his bag. We really didn't need John Wooden for a coach because we only played one game that year. It was only one game, but, oh boy, it was a game I shall never forget.

We were all very excited when Coach Martin told us we were to take a bus ride to Hallsville to play their 7th-8th grade team. The game plus the road trip were thrilling firsts for us. The fact that Hallsville was only 16 miles from Marshall did nothing to diminish our enthusiasm. For us, this was the big time. In the 1950s, most, if not all, Marshall seventh-graders had never played organized basketball. There were no youth leagues of any kind except for baseball. Couple our inexperience with the fact that most of us were so short getting the ball to the basket was more of a heave than a shot. At any rate, the two teams took the court and ran around on it in a style that barely resembled organized sports.

At halftime, we led 2–0 thanks to a lay-up I had made. It may sound like a baseball score, but it was seventh-grade basketball. Coach Martin gave us a rah-rah pep talk, and we went back out there for the certain-to-be exciting second half. The starting teams lined up for the ball toss at mid-court, the referee blew his whistle, and he tossed the ball for the jump. D. H. Martin won the toss and tapped the ball to me. I instantly dribbled off toward the basket and sunk an improbable lay-up. At that point, the ref went nuts on his whistle, and play was stopped. The ref called a conference with the scorer and the two coaches. After some discussion, it was determined that I had scored the basket at the wrong end of the court, and Hallsville was awarded the two points. If my teammates had known for sure what had just happened, they clearly would have teased me mercilessly. Fortunately, the chaos my wrong-way basket had caused had everyone scratching their heads. Play resumed, and the defensive struggle continued until D. H. made a basket, putting us ahead 4–2. Near the end of this thriller, I hit another lay-up – this time at the correct end of the court – giving us a lead of 6–2. That's the way the game ended. We won 6–2, and I went in the record books as having been the high scorer for both teams. When the dust settled, I took a lot of ribbing, which lasted for more than a week. I deserved it. Do you suppose my record has ever been tied?

After the disappointment of working our butts off for an entire seventh-grade basketball season to play only one game, we were stoked to start our eighth-grade basketball season. It was coached by the affable Coach Atwell, and we just knew we would play a full slate of games in front of an excitement-charged crowd. It turned out to be a near replay of our seventh-grade season. We played two games before a near-empty gym and went undefeated, but nobody cared. Two lousy games.

Junior high in the 1950s and 1960s covered grades seven through nine. Therefore, when you became a ninth-grader, you were at the top of the junior high heap. In athletics, it was your year to shine. We had a very good Mighty Mite varsity basketball team. Guy Martin was our best player. He and D. H. Martin were both over six-feet tall in the ninth-grade and were quite athletic. Guy had finesse and could shoot. D. H. had muscles and could rebound. I was our point guard, and Palmer Pratt and Paul Wood filled out our starting line-up. Paul was short on skill but overflowed with desire. His tank always registered "win at all costs." He was muscled up like D. H., and would-be rebounders just bounced off both. John Bogue and Roy Lee Fry were able substitutes who logged lots of playing time.

We played Texarkana for the district championship that year and went into the fourth quarter of that game with a three-point lead. According to an old newspaper clipping, a boy named Dicky James hit "a long one-hander in the final seconds" to defeat the Mighty Mites 22–21. That same article said I led the Mites in scoring with seven, followed by Guy with five – an off night for Guy.

One of the highlights of the season occurred during our last home game before the district tournament, when our official scorer, Bob Power, told Coach McNatt that everyone on the team had scored during the season except Stanley Skinner. Stanley was a lovable, hardworking country boy who was well overweight, causing him to be very slow at getting around on the court. His nickname was "Mole" because of his immobility and the fact that his cheeks were so chubby they filled his eye sockets to the point of reducing his vision range to mere slits. Coach McNatt wanted Stanley to break into the scoring column, so he put him into the game and told him to shoot every time he got the ball. Stanley got the message.

The first time he touched the ball, Stanley was just inside the half-court line. He surprised everyone in the gym because he didn't dribble down closer to the basket. Instead, the ambidextrous Stanley launched a high, arching, forty-foot, lefthanded hook shot that dropped right into the net for a goal. Coach nearly fainted, and everyone in the gym went wild. We all swamped Stanley and made him the hero of the game. "Mole" calmly turned toward Coach McNatt and made the "what's the big deal" sign with his upturned palms. Maybe Stanley should have played in more games. You go, Stanley. You go. A good season was over, but the memory lives on.

We had no junior high baseball team, so the only sport left for us ninth-graders was track in the spring. Track didn't seem to excite anyone, so very little about it took root in my memory. I do seem to remember that D. H. won the district discus toss, and Paul did very well in the shot-put competition, or vice versa. I ran the 100-yard dash but finished a not-so-hot sixth in the district. Palmer did pretty well in the hurdles. Bogue and I both competed in the broad jump, but neither of us took home any medals. Junior high sports were great fun, but they ended. High school sports were next, and we would have to start all over as rookies.

Frankly, high school sports weren't quite as much fun for me as junior high sports had been. Oh, I still enjoyed them and made lots of good memories, but athletics became so serious, the fun of the games waned a bit for me. I played no more football, but I managed to have a couple of good years in basketball and baseball. In baseball, Dicky Brassell, and I made Honorable Mention All-District. I mention this because I feel as though Dicky was slighted by not being named to First Team All-District as a pitcher, as his statistics ranked near the top of all pitching stats in our district. Honorable Mention was fine for me because I was no better than the third best shortstop in our conference. I was happy. I was offered a couple of small college scholarships in both basketball and baseball when I graduated, but I honestly felt my talent probably wasn't good enough to take me to the next level.

Chapter 06

Learning how to Cuss

There was, and still is, an art to cussing. Cursing, on the other hand, was a lot easier than cussing. It simply required the repeating of words that were considered "curse" words. They were used to show displeasure or, maybe, anger. Cussing, or more accurately called "cussin'," required facial expressions that fit the cuss word or words. Occasionally, a deadpan expression or raised eyebrows amplified the effectiveness of a story being laced with cuss words. It also had to be part of the story being told. It was tactically and artfully used to pique interest in what was being said. It added emphasis and color to the narrative and helped bring the story to life. A good cussin' out could painfully chop the legs out from under a fellow. Cussin' was verbal artistry, critical in creating a vision of what was being said. Cursing usually just made an ass of the curser; it just hung in the air and rang in the listener's ear long after it had been interjected into a conversation or sentence. Personally, I believe men from the South are better cussers than Northern men. The fellows from north of the Mason-Dixon line can curse with the best of swearers, but cussin' just doesn't sound right without a bit of Southern drawl to dress it up.

The need to write a chapter on the art of cussin' arose when I was reflecting on the vast number of changes many of us boys went through during our junior and senior high school years. As we struggled with trying to rush our manhood, cussin' was one of those things we had to learn how to do. Now is as good of a time as any to stress that many, if not most, boys in my age group did not feel it necessary to add the ability to cuss well to their repertoire as they progressed toward adulthood. I did.

Perhaps I considered the ability to cuss well as an asset because I came from a family of good cussers. Daddy, who was a spellbinding storyteller, always enlivened his stories with perfectly chosen cuss words interjected at the perfect times. Daddy was a first-ballot inductee in the Cussin' Hall of Fame. He didn't cuss all the time, just when he thought it served a purpose.

Daddy's oldest sister, Vina, was also in that hall of fame. She was a robust old gal who basically raised her eight siblings. Because of her rough, take-charge style, she picked up several nicknames along the way. Some called her "Sarge," for obvious reasons. Her youngest sister, Phyllis, dubbed her "Gil Favor" after the trail boss on the television show *Rawhide* (1957-1965). I well remember the time Aunt Vina showed up at our house with a beautiful Black Diamond watermelon. Upon entering the house, she told my brother, Robert, to bring the melon in from her 1953 Ford. Aunt Vina didn't make requests; she gave orders. When Robert retrieved the melon, he hoisted it to his right shoulder and headed for the front door. When he got to our small cement front porch, his foot slipped out from under him, and he went one way and the melon the other. We all heard the splat of the plump melon and raced to the front door to see what had happened. When Aunt Vina got there, she put her hands on her hips, stared down at the pitiful scene at her feet, and came out with the vilest "shit" ever uttered by mankind. Daddy often said, when Aunt Vina said, "shit," everyone in the room could smell it. I smelled it that day. Aunt Vina was so good at cussin' that Aunt Phyllis wrote a book about her verbal proclivities called *Satan's Angel*. It was written just for family members, so don't try to find it on Amazon.

Not everyone knows how to cuss. My brother Robert eventually learned to be a prolific and proficient cusser, but he was a slow learner. Once, when he was in the fifth grade, he got sent to the principal's office for ordering his milk in the cafeteria by calling it "bellywasher." Very few folks considered "bellywasher" a cuss word, but Robert's principal deemed it offensive. While that word wouldn't even draw a raised eyebrow today, it was considered "swearing" in 1947, at least by one cafeteria worker and a principal. The next year, Daddy got a call from Robert's principal ratting out my brother for saying, "shit dang." That offense earned Robert a session with Daddy that night, during which Daddy told Robert to either learn how to cuss properly or keep his mouth shut.

Daddy added that "shit dang" made no sense and sounded stupid. My Uncle Blackie was a very polished cusser, but he was interesting. There was something nice about his cussin'. He cussed softly, seldom ever raising his voice. His swear words sounded cute for some reason, maybe because he always raised his eyebrows to the max when he cussed.

It was like he had surprised himself by saying what he did. One of Uncle Blackie's favorite sayings was, "I'll be go to hell." It made absolutely no sense, but it was oddly effective. Not all cussin' made sense. Daddy often referred to someone he didn't care for as a "son of a biscuit eater." Obviously, it was a sanitized version of son-of-a-bitch. Kudos to Pop for conveying his nasty thoughts in a more pleasant way.

It took some doin' to build your cuss word vocabulary. I didn't know but four or five swear words until I got to junior high. Then, they started piling up rather quickly. The most new-to-me swear words I ever heard in one session occurred one night at a Marshall Lion's Club fish fry. My best friend Terry's dad was a member of the Lion's Club. He invited me to accompany him and Terry to the Lion's Father-Son Fish Fry that was held on fellow Lion Ernest Smith's farm.

While the Lions were preparing all the food and enjoying their beer, a group of their sons and sons' friends gathered for talking and telling jokes. Terry and I were among the youngest. We were about twelve years old at the time, and we stood quietly by as Joe Black, a savvy fourteen-year-old, told dirty joke after dirty joke to his enthralled audience. To this day, I've never met a man who could rattle off as many jokes as Joe could. Terry and I laughed at all the jokes even though many were well beyond our comprehension. Joe had a knack for joke-telling and, that night, he introduced many, many, new swear words for us to learn to use. Incidentally, I never heard the dreaded f-word until I was in junior high. Its use didn't become commonplace until I was well into my adult years. I wonder how many kids today make it to seventh-grade before hearing it? "Fart" and "pissed-off" have now been so normalized, one hears them regularly on prime-time television. This was not so in the '50s and '60s.

I've always felt as though cursing was cussin' with a suit and tie on. Cursing seems to be okay at a civil party, the country club, or at the Senior Prom, while, in Marshall, cussin' was something you did at Rayford's Garage or in the men's room at the Paramount Theater. If you were a pipe smoker, you were a curser. If you chewed tobacco or smoked Camels, you were a cusser. I'm not an advocate of cursing or cussin'. As a matter of fact, I do a fair amount of cringing when in the company of one prone to excessively "colorful" language. However, in the spirit of honesty, I confess having a certain amount of admiration for a fellow who knows how to artfully adorn a good story with a few well-chosen cuss words. If you made it to manhood without developing your cussin' potential, I'm proud of you and for you. Well done. I didn't, dammit.

Chapter 07

Be Still My Heart

I have always been a dedicated observer of all girls and an admirer of many of them. However, I write this chapter on girls with fear and trepidation. I fear that readers might think I was obsessed with girls, and I am trepiditious about listing the names of the girls I found so pretty in junior and senior high school.

I was NOT obsessed with girls in junior and senior high school! At least I don't think I was. Sure, I liked girls a lot during those years in junior and senior high school, but obsessed? No way. Oh hell, I confess to being obsessed with girls back then. In my defense, I confidently assert that nearly every boy I knew back then suffered from the same obsession. Puberty had entered our bodies like bucking broncs and, while we tried to rein it in, it reared, snorted, kicked, and bucked at times of its own choosing, often when we wished it hadn't. It would be a while before we "broke" the stallion known as puberty and gained control of it. You know, I truly wish I knew what girls were thinking back then. Did they have the same urges and longings, but simply controlled them better?

I am now wading into the shark-infested waters that come with naming some of the girls I thought were knock-outs back then. Have you ever known doing a certain thing was stupid, but you did it anyway? I am throwing caution and good sense to the wind and naming names. It is a certainty that I will inadvertently leave some beautiful girls' names off the list. If you were left off my list and were good-looking and knew it, please accept my apology. I assure you your omission was due to my hit-and-miss memory.

We had pretty girls in South Marshall Elementary School but, honestly, it wasn't that big of a deal. Recess, baseball cards, and little league baseball were higher on my list of priorities than girls. Things changed once we got to junior high. Thanks to falling under the all-powerful spell of puberty and a dramatic new concentration of girls that had previously been scattered among the five other elementary schools in Marshall, I spent a lot of time staring and wishing. As we boys clumsily stumbled our ways toward manhood, the girls were taking noticeable steps toward becoming women. By the ninth-grade, it looked to me like the girls had about completed their metamorphosis into womanhood. The butterflies were shedding their cocoons and filling my environment with beauty and grace. I was enthralled.

Ninth-grade was a pivotal year for me when it came to girls. Girls I had grown up with like Lynn Abney, Dolly DeBeaux, and Carol Marshall went from cute to gorgeous. Wow! When I looked behind me at the seventh and eighth-grade girls, I saw beautiful females like Pam Allison, Nancy Morris, Sharon Wright, Becky Shoults, Marion Wright, and Sandra Maddox. When I glimpsed the high schoolers ahead of me, I was awestruck by what I thought was the most beautiful collection of women God ever put on earth. As an aside, I'm not sure I wasn't right on target with my tenth-grade assessment. I guess you had to have been there.

When I finally became a tenth grader, our first year of high school back then, I couldn't believe I was actually walking the halls with Annabelle Holcomb, Linda Graves, Jo Lynne Beckett, Kay Blackmon, Lynn Newman, Nan Scott, Grace Ann Amidon, Narcie and Narcissa Moore, Pat Muse, Simmie Mullikin, Martha Ingram, etc., etc. In my case, they added up to a severe case of sensory overload.

Another vexing challenge I faced in writing this chapter about girls was what to say about the ones I dated in junior and senior high. I would like to pay homage to those young ladies without revealing any items that might cause embarrassment, lawsuits, or ruffled feathers. My solution? I will simply list them here and totally avoid any details of our relationships: Seventh-grade - Carol Marshall and Susan Cacioppo; Eighth-grade - Susan Cacioppo; Ninth-grade - Diane Whitis; Tenth-grade - Sharon Wright; Eleventh-grade - Sharon Wright and Kay Campbell; Twelfth grade - Kay Campbell

In between these "going steady" relationships, I had fun dates with several girls including Lynn Abney, Judy Ford, Dona Gale Gary, Becky Shoults, Sharon Carey, Dolly DeBeaux, and a hand full of out-of-towners.

Now, all silliness and efforts at humor aside, all of these girls were terrific individuals with generous souls and strong character. I respected them then, and I still do. They each still own a tiny piece of my heart.

I mentioned above that I had a date with Dolly DeBeaux. Dolly and I had been in elementary school together so our friendship pre-dated high school. She was one of those girls who got better and better looking each year. Her ascension up the beauty ladder culminated with her being voted Most Beautiful our senior year. At the time of our date, she was actually "going with" a good friend of mine, Jimmy Elliott. The two of them were slated to go on a hayride together, but Jimmy had to go out of town. Jimmy didn't want Dolly to have to miss the hayride so he asked me if I would mind taking her in his stead. Since they were both friends, I agreed to fill in for him. Truth is, I was kind of proud he trusted me enough to ask me to do so. When I picked Dolly up, she looked great in a pair of wheat-colored Levis and a long-sleeved white shirt. She didn't just look great, she looked really, really, really great, and she smelled wonderful. I always noticed Dolly's mother smelled heavenly whenever I rode home from school with them. Believe me when I tell you, the DeBeaux gals had mastered the art of smelling good. Excuse my digression.

When we boarded the hay wagon, we found a spot right up next to the truck's cab and wiggled ourselves into a comfortable position. Instantly, I liked being next to Dolly. However, I also instantly felt the weight of the trust Jimmy had laid on me. That entire darned hayride started off with me in conflict with my urges. It was a cool autumn night so, naturally, Dolly and I cuddled up a bit to share the warmth. Her nearness, her perfume, and the beauty of the night assaulted my loyalty to Jimmy, and Dolly and I started with a little kiss, then another, and another, and another. Oh my, you get the picture. At that moment, I was hoping Jimmy would stay gone a couple of months, but I knew he would be back in two days. Phooey. The thought of his return, which was probably going through Dolly's mind, too, turned the world's greatest hayride into just a cold ride in the back of a flatbed truck. I was in love with Dolly for about 45 minutes, but when the hayride was over, we went back to just being friends.

Just this year, Jimmy and I were visiting at a family get-together (we married cousins), and I told him of the dilemma he had put me in with Dolly. He just laughed. He should have thanked me for my loyalty to our friendship. He didn't. He just laughed.

As I wrote about Dolly smelling so good, I thought of another "smell good" story. If you read the above chart about who I dated when, you noticed I dated a cute little redhead named Kay Campbell a year and a half. It was customary back then to give your high school sports letter jacket to your steady. Kay had – and wore – mine for a long time. It was also customary to return your beau's jacket when the relationship ended. Kay did return my jacket, and it was stored away for nearly 50 years. When I went through a clean-out/throw-out program, I ran across my letter jacket. While it was now too small for me, it treated me to many near-forgotten sports and dating memories. The amazing thing was that after 50 years, it still smelled like Kay Campbell. I don't remember which perfume or cologne Kay wore, but it took the blue ribbon for endurance. Today, there's some bum walking around Phoenix, Arizona, in a Marshall High School letter jacket smelling like Kay Campbell.

Throughout my first book, *Mad Dogs, Marbles, and Rock Fights,* and this one, too, I've talked about my friendship with Lynn Abney. Lynn and I had a complex relationship. I think we were always pretty close, but as we matured, our friendship intensified and our closeness became tinged with a bit of electricity we felt for each other. The fact that both of us were always dating other people did not interfere with our spending time together. Many, many afternoons after school, Terry Weeks, John Bogue, David Wist and I went to the Abney's house to play cards and share time. Mrs. Abney and Lynn's younger sisters, Kackie and Barbara, became like family to us. While the card games were fun, I really just wanted to be with Lynn. A little bit of hugging and kissing occasionally went on between us for years, but we never really dated.

The primo party givers in our class were Lynn and Carol Marshall. Lynn's parties were usually slumber parties. Boys were allowed to hang around until about midnight, at which time Mrs. Abney would run us off. One night, I decided to hide from Mrs. Abney in the closet in the Abney's den. My plan, which Lynn sanctioned, was to hide in the closet until Mrs. Abney locked up and went to bed. The hide-a-bed in Lynn's den accommodated three girls, one of whom was Lynn. She was supposed to free me from the closet when her mom went upstairs. Good plan. Poor execution. The closet had a slatted door, so I could hear as Mrs. Abney made her final boy-check. It was very dark in the closet so I never had a chance to scope it out before Lynn closed me up inside. Really dumb.

Well, when Mrs. Abney told the girls good night and headed for the stairs, I knew I had it made. In silent celebration, I stiffened my right arm and leaned to my right thinking my right hand would hit the wall and prevent me from falling. Again, really dumb. I assumed the closet was normal sized. It wasn't. It was a large walk-in closet and my hand never hit the wall. Instead, I went straight to the floor where – are you ready for this? – the Abneys stored their empty Coke bottles waiting to be redeemed for three cents each. The noise of the bottles banging into each other on the closet's tile floor was deafening and seemed to go on forever. It sounded like a busy bowling alley on league night. When the noise finally stopped, and I regained my senses, the door slowly opened to reveal a frowning Mrs. Abney, with both hands on her hips, staring down at me. The girls were all giggling as Mrs. Abney marched me to the front door. This is as good of a place as any for me to talk about Mrs. Abney. To me, she was top drawer all the way. She always made my friends and me feel like we were special to her. I know she must have had days when she looked out her window, saw us pull up at her curb, and said, "Oh Lord, don't those boys have a home to go to?" She never, and I mean never, made us feel anything but welcome at her house. Thank you, Helen Abney.

My dad was in the insurance business, and he preferred to work the smaller towns and cities of East Texas. His modus operandi was to distribute information pamphlets about his insurance to every house in a small town. There was a pre-paid postage mail response card that those interested in being contacted to learn more about the insurance could drop in the mail. Those cards came to Dad who, in turn, made appointments with the responders. The positive responses usually were enough to fill a week's worth of work. I've dragged you through that rural marketing plan to tell you that Daddy hired John Bogue and me to distribute his pamphlets to all the homes in Avinger, Texas. Avinger was a small town located between the slightly larger East Texas towns of Jefferson and Hughes Springs.

John and I would work a street together. He put response cards on the front doors of houses on one side of the street, and I did the same on the other side. Everything went according to plan until I walked up on the front porch of a small frame house that had seen better days.

There were no leash laws in those days, so dogs had free run of their worlds. About the only dogs that got tied up were those with rabies or those that were threats to eat small children. With this in mind, I wasn't the least bit worried about the ancient hound I saw sprawled next to the railing on the front porch. He was so lifeless, I wondered if he was dead or just in the process of dying. He looked like an old bloodhound. He had huge tan ears, large rheumy, bloodshot eyes, and wrinkles on his wrinkles. There was little meat on his bones, just skin loosely covering what was once muscle. I was mesmerized by the creature and bent down to study it and to wish it well in dog heaven. As I knelt down, he arched one eyebrow as if to check me out. Then, to my surprise, he stretched out his front legs and - if I didn't know better - I would've sworn he pulled himself up by hanging on to the porch railing. He then turned his unsteady swaybacked body to me, took one step toward me, gave out one pitiful bark, and bit the hell out of me. He then collapsed onto the porch floor and never looked at me again. I was shocked, but the bite was pretty much painless. I just continued to stare at him, thinking that some thought must have flickered in his brain reminding him that he was a watchdog. I had just received the last bit of watch-doggin' he had left in him. I was proud of him.

Before I leave my "young boy-meets-old dog" story, I am going to interject a few of my observations about the differences between city dogs and country dogs. There's probably no scientific basis for the conclusions I'm about to offer, but I've drawn them through keen observation and memorable experiences. In thinking about the differences between city dogs and country dogs, it occurred to me that those differences may also be found between city folks and country folks.

The first difference I've noted between city dogs and country dogs is the amount of energy they expend in going about their business. A city dog generally clips through life at a much faster pace than does his rural cousin. He seems to think he has more to do, so he is usually in a hurry. The country dog slow-drags his feet as he walks toward his destination. The city dog keeps his head up in the "alert" position, while the country dog hangs his head as though he's just looking for his next place to lie down. The energetic city dog keeps his tail pointing skyward. The country dog drags his tail as though it weighs ten pounds. I've often wondered if the country dog is just creeping through life because it is saving its energy for a rabbit or squirrel that may cross its path. Maybe it thinks it might have to go from zero to 60 if called upon to catch something wild. Reckon? When a city dog is tired, it just lies down and catnaps. When a country dog is overwhelmed by a case of the sleepies, it circles around its chosen location repeatedly until it decides it is, in fact, the perfect spot to crash. The slightest noise or movement will cause the city dog to perk-up and determine what happened. The country dog falls into a deep sleep and sometimes has to be roused-up with a nudge. City dogs bark more than country dogs. The sound of their bark is sharper, and it often gets on the listener's nerves because it sounds yappier. Country dogs are stingier with their barks, and, in East Texas, they clearly bark with a Southern drawl. Their barks just fizzle out while city dogs clip theirs off. All dogs – and humans - like their bellies rubbed. A city dog will rollover once you've calmed it. A country dog rolls over if it even suspects you might rub its belly. A city dog licks you if he likes you. A country dog nudges you if he likes you. Rural and city dogs will bite. However, the city dog usually warns you a bite is coming. The country dog often ambles up to you and bites without a warning. Country dogs are fractious if they are indoors. City dogs panic if they are outdoors and lose sight of their master. Country dogs are quite entertaining when they try to gain traction on linoleum floors. They are used to having dirt underfoot, not a slick surface.

I hope this tutorial on city dogs versus country dogs has enlightened some of you urbanites. Even if it doesn't, I've enjoyed writing it. By the way, I prefer the company of country dogs.

Are you wondering how my "old dog on the porch" story fits into a chapter on girls? Well it does. Listen. When the lady of the house heard the yelp of her old hound, she opened the front door and found me standing there. She quickly pieced the preceding drama together and asked me if Old Cal had bothered me. I filled her in on his last effort to protect her, and she just chuckled. She told me Cal didn't have enough teeth or jaw strength to hurt anyone, but it made him feel good to bite strangers. She insisted I come in for a glass of cold water, which I eagerly did. She had me sit on her sofa while she fetched my water. When she returned from the kitchen, the plot thickened. She sat opposite me and began to tell me about her granddaughter who had just graduated from Avinger High School. She was selling hard and told me her granddaughter had been voted Most Intelligent, Most Popular, and Most Beautiful by her classmates. I'd be lying to you if I said she hadn't piqued my interest. She went on to tell me I should come back in about an hour as her granddaughter would be at the house by then. It was obvious she was hoping to hook the girl up with this "city" boy from Marshall. I agreed to come meet her and rushed out to tell John my good news.

I showed up at the house at the appointed time, steered wide of Old Cal, and knocked on the door. Granny opened it and invited me in where she introduced me to her granddaughter, Wanda Ann. Grandma then found an excuse to exit the room, leaving Wanda Ann and me to "spark." The young lady was embarrassed, and I was taken aback. Now, let me tell you why I was taken aback. I was not handsome, but I had not been voted Most Handsome. Wanda Ann was not beautiful, but she had been voted Most Beautiful. She was not beautiful, not even close. Was I being pranked? The more she and I talked, the more I realized she was smart and did have a wonderful personality. She earned those votes, but I was still shaken by her modest looks. After getting to know each other, I shared with her that her granny told me about the honors she had won in high school. Wanda Ann blushed and asked me if granny had told me there were only three girls in her graduating class. No, she hadn't. Once again, my own stupidity and naivety had got me into a sticky situation. Why didn't it dawn on me that Avinger was so tiny it couldn't have had many girls in the senior class? She went on to tell me her senior class just kind of divided up the "favorite" elections so as to avoid hurting anyone's feelings. Well done Avinger. I will confess that I wondered what those other two girls looked like if Wanda Ann was the prettiest of the three.

I learned a few things that day, though. Just because an old dog looks harmless, don't assume it is harmless; if something sounds too good to be true, it probably is; and, you don't have to be pretty to be beautiful. I got to know Wanda Ann pretty well that day. She really was beautiful on the inside, and that's what counts the most. Wanda Ann would have received my vote for Most Beautiful, too.

I've shared most all of my stories about girls that are fit for print, but I would be remiss if I didn't admit that teen-aged boys also occasionally fall for grown women. I did. One afternoon, Terry, Mickey, John, and I drove around Marshall looking for something new to do. As we passed the nearly vacant Harrison County Airport, we noticed a sign that said the lobby restaurant was open for business. This was a revelation for us because we had no commercial air service and very little general aviation. We decided to try out the place and in we marched. The only people in the small restaurant were the waitress and the cook, both of whom sat in a booth chatting away. We grabbed a booth, and they stirred into action. The waitress came to our table and the cook headed for the kitchen.

When I looked at the waitress, it was love at first sight. We ordered Cokes and, when she brought them to our table, she stood there talking to us for some time. Her attention to us was not because we were overly impressive. It was because she was overly bored. She pulled up a chair and, soon thereafter, called the cook to join us. The six of us had a lot of fun and shared lots of laughs. We had found something new to do in Marshall on lazy afternoons and new friends to do it with. It became a near-daily visit everyone seemed to enjoy. First, there was Joyce, who

was a waitress, a really pretty black-haired lady who I'd guess was in her late thirties. She was well-shaped and, perhaps unknowingly, had a mildly provocative way of moving and talking – at least I thought so;
then came Australia, a cook with a round, jovial face who laughed easily and was fun to talk with. Once in a while, she baked us a pie, and she and Joyce would let us eat it without charging us for it. She was a really good cook. We just never had enough money to buy more than Cokes.

My crush on Joyce grew daily, and I even reached the point where I thought she might have developed some feelings for me. That romance I was building in my imagination came tumbling down one day when a lineman for a local utility company came into the restaurant and hugged and kissed "my" Joyce. She lit up with happiness upon his arrival and brought him over to our table for introductions. She also told us they were to be married as soon as his divorce was finalized. We continued to visit Joyce and Australia for a while longer, and we even got to know and like her fiancé, but we soon lost interest. We decided it was time to find something new to do to break the boredom of a Marshall afternoon. I hope Joyce and her man lived happily for many, many years.

I must have had a thing for waitresses, because the next adult lady I fell for was the waitress at Smoke's Smokehouse Café on Highway 43. I never knew her first name, just that she was Mrs. Smoke. She ran the small barbecue place that she and her husband Bill owned. Bill was a Marshall policeman, so he was seldom at the café. Most of my visits to Smoke's were with Ronnie McMullen. We shared a taste for barbecue and for Mrs. Smoke. She was a curvaceous, smallish lady with raven-black hair that hung to her mid-back. She looked to be in her late 20s to early 30s. She was pretty and looked like she should have been a country and western singer. She dressed like one, too. Ronnie and I flirted with her relentlessly. She was pleasant about our efforts but not encouraging. Officer Bill stopped by the café several times when we were there. I suspect he was cognizant of our infatuation with his wife, but I don't think he was worried about our wooing his wife away from him. Perhaps realizing the futility of our romantic interests, Ronnie and I decided it probably wasn't the smartest thing to be flirting with the wife of a man who wears a gun. The romance was gone from this wanna-be relationship. No matter. There were lots of pretty females in Marshall.

I have great memories of the girls (and women) of Marshall. If I was re-incarnated as the biblical King Solomon, I would come to Marshall to select my 1,000 wives.

Chapter 08

God, May I have Gravy with my Manna?

Wikipedia defines gravy as "a sauce often made from the juices of meats that run naturally during cooking and may be thickened with flour or cornstarch for added texture." Something else I read about gravy said it is "a product of scarcity and ingenuity." The formal definition is accurate, but the latter description hits closer to home with me. There's no doubt in my mind that Mom and Dad fed my two big, robust, older brothers and me lots of foods designed to fill us up without completely depleting their modest bankroll. We were difficult to fill up, so our parents were in constant pursuit of meaningful fillers to put on our plates. Gravy was the most common of the fillers at our house, although we didn't know it was a filler. We thought of it as a special treat. In fact, I would have been happy if Mom or Dad had just stirred up a skillet full of gravy and turned me loose on it with a straw.

My dad was the head gravy chef at our house, and he was a master at whipping up a batch of cream gravy, brown gravy, red-eye ham gravy, roast beef red-eye gravy, and several other kinds of gravy that had no names. My mom's red tomato-based gravy was her specialty, and it always accompanied her incredible meatloaf. We ate gravy on mashed potatoes, rice, biscuits, white bread, and meat. My brothers and I fought for the right to sop up the gravy remnants left in the pan or skillet. I truly miss my parents' gravy. It was superbly delicious.

When I was six or eight years old, I told my brother, Robert, how much I loved gravy. He, in turn, asked me what food I most liked to put in on. I told him I liked it over my mashed potatoes. He agreed with my choice and went on to tell me it tasted great on all kinds of potatoes. Made sense to me. He then told me I should put gravy on my potato chips if I wanted a taste of Heaven. I tried Mother's red meatloaf gravy on a bowl full of potato chips the next night, and it was terrible, like throw-up inducing terrible. It was disappointing to learn that even gravy had its limitations.

If you were raised in the South, you learned to love chicken fried steaks. It was – and is – impossible to eat chicken fried steaks without covering it with white gravy. In high school, lots of boys rendezvoused at the Ranch House, a run-down truck stop on Highway 80, after dates or parties for a late-night chicken fried steak drenched in gravy. The Ranch House, which surely pre-dated health department inspections, and the café in the Ginocchio Hotel both served tasty chicken fried steaks and stayed open late. I preferred the old hotel because the night cook was a dear old gal named Rosalee. Rosalee had worked for us several years when I was a little boy. To an extent, I had been raised on Rosalee's cooking and caring hugs. When I went to the Ginocchio, I would go into the kitchen to pay my respects to Rosaleee and get a hug. If she sized me up and decided I had been drinking beer, she made me drink several cups of coffee before sending me on my way.

Even today, Kay and I still treat ourselves to gravy-covered chicken fried steaks at least once every week or two at Randy's Café in Scottsdale. Randy's is an island from the past in the heart of the chic, urbane, and bustling Scottsdale that seems to "call us home" for pleasant encounters with waiters and waitresses that still appreciate a 15% tip and blue-plate specials that harken back to the 1950s. We send cholesterol on vacation on those occasions while we savor these gravy-rich reminders of our past. Of course, the Arizona version of chicken fried steaks may not measure up to those we had in East Texas, but they suffice and trigger taste bud delights and fond food memories.

When my friend, David Wist, took a job in Kansas City before he was married, he asked an attractive young lady out for dinner. She accepted. David could tell this girl was a simple country girl not yet savvy to the ways of the city, so when they were seated at the elegant restaurant he had selected, he noted her confusion with the snobby menu. Being the gentleman he has always been, David suggested he order for both of them. She gladly accepted his suggestion. David ordered two nice steaks for them, thinking he had baled her out of an embarrassing predicament. However, the waiter threw him a curve by asking his date how she wanted her steak prepared. Before David could answer for her, the flummoxed young lady responded with the only answer she could come up with. She looked at the waiter and answered, "chicken fried." Bless her little old pea-picking Southern heart. Many years ago, a Southern boy told me that if you pierced the ears of the girls in his hometown, gravy would come out. I don't doubt him at all.

Gravy had its heyday before doctors took the fun out of eating it by branding it as cholesterol-rich and toxic to one's heart. Damn. Because I'm now trying to extend my life, I don't eat much gravy these days. I can't stand the image it creates in my mind of my major blood vessels slamming shut with cholesterol-induced blood flow stoppers. The guilt sucks. You know that old saying, "ignorance is bliss?" I think it describes my relationship with gravy before the doctors nixed it. I enjoyed gravy a whole lot more when the eating of it was guilt-free, but doing anything guilt-free is rare these days. Bummer.

I suspect kids from wealthier families didn't eat as much gravy as our family did. Their families probably didn't need budget-stretching fillers like gravy. I need to ask some of my classmates who were raised in well-to-do families about that. Gravy was darn near a meal unto itself. If gravy was something only the poor ate, well, poverty wasn't all that bad. Now that I think of it, I feel sorry for those who grew up in gravy-starved families. Gravy without money is tolerable. Money without gravy isn't. I'd be willing to bet you that if medical science hadn't put the whammy on gravy, there would be a chain of fast food gravy stores today to rival McDonald's.

The French got really good at making gravy back when they needed something to disguise the taste of the inferior meat they served. In typical French style, they refused to call their flavorful liquid "gravy." They dubbed it "sauce", thinking, I suppose, "gravy" was too plebian for anything French. It worked, because the French became famous for their "marvelous" sauces. It even became acceptable to overpay for meals covered by their sauces. As I see it, you serve gravy when you need something to put on top of inferior food that will divert attention away from its poor quality, you need filler because you don't have – or can't afford –enough food to fill yourself or those seated around your table, you understand that most everyone loves gravy, or you just like to show-off your culinary skills.

When I was a little boy, I asked my mother what God fed the people in Heaven. Mother thought for a minute and then replied, "it's called manna."

I, in turn, thought for a minute and responded, "Momma, when I'm in heaven, can I get gravy with my manna?" Mother smiled, nodded, and changed the subject. If there is a God – and I know there is – He'll have gravy on hand for us Southern Christians. Amen.

Chapter 09

Never the Hero, Often the Goat

Sports stories usually feature the stars doing heroic things. Not this one. It's about a boy – me – who flirted with sports heroics but repeatedly found ways to blow it.

Most boys grow up dreaming of being the guy who hits the game-winning homerun, scores the winning bucket as the game-ending buzzer goes off, or crosses the goal line with the winning touchdown on the last play of the game.

Scotty Eubanks, A Proud Maverick in 1962

I played lots of sports – football, basketball, baseball and track – and I was well above average at each of them. It would only make sense that I wore the hero's crown at least once during my "star-studded" career. Surely, my hit won an important baseball game, even if only in Little League. I must have – somewhere along the line – hit the winning bucket in a basketball game. Surely.

Well, I've got to be honest. I cannot recall even one time I left the court or field as the hero. I can, however, remember several times when my error or foul caused us to lose a game we should have won. I have always heard bad sports memories out-live good ones. Seems so.

The last year of my Little League experience, I was the second-best pitcher in the National League. Palmer Pratt was the best. One night, we were playing the Cardinals. It was a game we, the Giants, needed to win to stay tied with Palmer's Dodgers in first place. Jerry Scott had pitched for us, and we were ahead 8–7, needing only one more out to secure the victory. Jerry walked the next two batters, and they went to third and second on a wild pitch. Our coach, Tommy Moore, called time out, went to the mound, and brought me in from third base to replace Jerry and to get that all-important third out. After all, I was our ace. I finished my warm-up tosses, and the umpire, Mr. James Timms, hollered, "Play ball!"

The batter I was to face was Bob Faust. I wasn't worried, thinking I could strike Bob out. The drama – and my chance to be a hero – ended with the first pitch. Bob hit it hard to right-center field, and both runs scored easily. We lost. Bob was swarmed by all his teammates and coaches. They were beside themselves with joy. Bob was the hero. I had blown it. My teammates and I ambled off the field with our chins on our chests. There was no joy in Mudville that night. We stayed in a funk until Leslie Lawrence announced that his parents were buying everyone on the Giants a snow cone. I think that act of generosity chased away the angst caused by the bitter loss for everyone but me. I still dream about that pitch, and I'll bet Bob Faust does, too.

When the all-stars were named at the end of that season, I was on the team. We won our first game, with Palmer Pratt pitching us to victory over Gladewater. That victory advanced us to the next round, where we faced our arch rivals, the vaunted Longview All Stars. I was chosen to pitch that game. I held them to two hits, and we were leading 4–2 going into the last inning. I promptly walked the first two batters, putting the tying and winning runs on base. Both runners moved up a base on a groundout to first. I walked another batter, and I struck out the next hitter. Just one out to go. I could taste the victory. The Longview coach sent a pinch hitter named Lonnie Watley to the plate. Lonnie ended my dreams of being a hero by clobbering my first pitch into centerfield, scoring the tying runs. The next batter hit my next pitch to the same place Watley had hit his, driving in the winning run. Bummer. Once again, I came very close to being hailed as a hero, only to walk off the field as the goat.

After Little League, boys moved up to the Babe Ruth League. It was for ages thirteen through fifteen. I made the all-stars when I was fourteen and fifteen, and when I was fifteen, we had a very good all-star team. We won a couple of games, advancing us to play Texarkana for the right to go to Austin for the Texas championship tournament. The Texarkana pitcher, Jodie Burkett, threw a no-hitter against us, but we won the game 2–1. I drove in one of our runs with a sacrifice fly and scored our winning run on a last inning passed ball. Ronnie McMullen pitched a three-hitter for us. At any rate, I was sort of a hero. Right?

Well, anyway, we were off to Austin and the state championship tournament!

The hotels and motels in Austin were filled by teams and their fans (mostly family members) from all over the Lone Star State. We stayed at an old-timey tourist court called the San Jose Motel out on the Old San Antonio Highway. To us kids, this was the big time. I had led our league in hitting for the entire season, so I, along with others, had great expectations for myself. Well, as fate would have it, I woke up the morning of our first game with a severe case of bronchitis, bordering on asthma. When I wasn't sneezing, I was blowing my nose. When I wasn't coughing, I was trying to focus my watery eyes. I was sick and running a fever; but I played. I played, but I didn't play well. No matter. We won. D. H. Martin pitched a shutout for us as we beat Graham, Texas, 8–0. I went hitless in three at-bats and was the only starter not to have a hit. Yuck.

Next, we beat a good Wharton team behind Ronnie's McMullen's strong pitching and Eddie's Green's two-run triple. David Gragg and Jerry Scott got a bunch of hits for us. I sneezed, snorted, coughed, and blew my way to a dismal 0 for 4 performance. I weakly grounded out to the infield all four times. No matter. We won.

We won a third game, but I can't remember who we beat. I do remember going hitless in two officials at bats. I walked twice, but, once again, no hits. I was still sick. No matter. We won.

In the semi-finals, we went up against a powerful team of Austin all-stars. They had blown away all their competition so far, and, being the hometown team, they owned the crowd. We battled them hard, and, as I recall, they beat us in a squeaker, 5–4. I was still sick and played like it. I capped off a perfect hitless tournament with a 0 for 3. The league's top hitter – yours truly – had gone hitless in twelve at-bats. Clutch performance, huh? Austin went on to easily win the state championship, and we took third place. By the way, the game had to be stopped in the second inning because a black cloud of gnats descended on the field and severely hampered our ability to see or breathe. It took about an hour, but the City of Austin sent trucks loaded with DDT to spray the area. The gnats had enough sense to retreat to Lake Austin. We didn't. We breathed in the DDT and played on.

In high school, I wasn't close to being the best hitter on our team. That honor was shared by Butch Kennedy, Danny Love, Deacon Lewis and D. H. Martin. I was considered a very good fielding shortstop, and

I took great pride in it. I felt no pressure at all when my hitting hovered around mediocrity. I guess I had become a fielder, not a hitter.

My sophomore year, we ended our regular season tied with John Tyler High School atop the district standings, necessitating a play-off game to see which team advanced to the regionals. The big game was played on a neutral field, one in Henderson, Texas, as I recall. The starting line-ups were announced over the public-address system, and when they introduced me, they added that I had just been named as the "best fielding shortstop in Texas." Danny Love came over to me from his second base position and asked me about this announcement. I told him I had heard nothing about such an honor. I didn't tell him I was as proud as a peacock for the honor, just that I knew nothing of it. I never heard another word about this wonderful honor, so I really don't know if it was true or if the p.a. announcer was just a big fan of mine. That day, I just bathed myself in the glory of the announcement, playing it over and over in my mind.

In the last inning of that game, I got a real lesson in how God humbles the prideful. The game was tied 4–4, but John Tyler had the bases loaded with only one out. Coach Story pulled our infield in on the grass so we could cut off the go-ahead run on a groundball. Deacon fired a strike, and the batter managed to hit a soft, sinking line drive right to me, the "best fielding shortstop in Texas." Easy play, right? Not that day. To me, the soft liner looked like it was coming at me at one hundred miles per hour. I was deceived by its off-speed, and the meekly-hit ball bounced off my chest. It never even touched my glove. I was able to throw out the hitter, but the go-ahead run scored on my misplayed ball. We lost 5–4. Once again, I had achieved stardom in the world of sports goats. Yeah, Scott. You rock.

I didn't limit my sports bloopers to baseball. I dribbled my way into basketball infamy several times in high school. Lufkin proved to be a hard place for me to put it all together on the hardwood. I scored quite a few points against the Panthers, but other issues often arose that overshadowed my accomplishments. We were engaged in a nip-and-tuck battle with Lufkin one night in their gym, and some pushing and shoving broke out between our teams over some disputed foul calls. Our Coach, Harold Tilley, had been assessed a double technical foul for getting in the referee's face over one of the calls, and his anger had spread to everyone in the gym, the Panthers' fans included. Those fans were screaming insults at us, and they started throwing coins at us from the bleachers. Those coins hurt like the dickens when they hit us. Each one that landed felt like a bee sting. The refs stopped the game several times in attempts to restore order. While the Lufkin coach made a plea for calm over the public address system, our guard, Don Ballard, was hustling around the court, picking up the coins that had been hurled at us, and cramming them in his socks. I guess things were tough at the Ballard house. On the bus ride home, Don told me the Lufkin crowd was cheap, adding that he only found pennies and nickels as he scoured the floor. It was a tough night all the way around for the boys from Marshall.

Any moment of calm inspired by the Lufkin coach lasted only until play resumed. Their bleachers ran down almost to the edge of the playing floor. That fact is worth understanding because it played into the following drama. I was dribbling the ball along the edge of the court toward the Lufkin basket when, all at once, one of the Panthers' fans moved to court's edge and stuck out his leg in an attempt to trip me. In response, I forgot all about the ball, and grabbed his leg, and yanked him onto the floor, and dropped my knee into his chest. Other fans came to his rescue and, ultimately, managed to throw me about three or four rows into the stands. While trying to rejoin the skirmish, I noticed my head had landed in the lap of a very pretty co-ed, but I digress. The melee soon spread like wildfire and threatened to erupt into a maul-the-Mavericks event, when a slew of Lufkin policemen and teachers managed to bring order to the chaos. Many fans were escorted out of the gym, and both teams were sequestered in their respective locker rooms for a cooling off period. Thank God. We were vastly outnumbered and would have been ground into mincemeat if a riot had developed.

When we returned to the playing court, our teams met in the middle, and shook hands, and agreed to return to civility. I wish they had called the game and sent us home to Marshall. Here's why. We were ahead by one point, thanks to a Guy Martin or Ronnie Ward field goal, and there were only three seconds left on the clock. Lufkin called a timeout. During that timeout, Coach Tilley told us we had it won if we just didn't foul. They didn't have time to go the full length of the court and score in only three seconds. He looked each one of us in the eye and said, "Don't foul!" Lufkin passed the ball in, and their guy started a mad, but futile, effort to dribble far enough down the court to launch a Hail Mary. We were going to win, but…..but, guess what? I fouled their dribbler. With one second left on the clock, he sunk both ends of a one and one. We lost. Eubanks had snatched defeat from the jaws of victory. Hero? Nope. Goat? You betcha. We had to have a police escort to our bus after the game, and our bus had to have a police escort to the Lufkin city limits.

Later that basketball season, we traveled to Sherman, Texas, to play in a prestigious tournament at Austin College. Lots of college coaches were known to visit this tournament because of the large number of high school stars who were on hand. We went to Sherman the day before our first game, and I hooked up with David Thomas, a friend from Marshall who was on a football scholarship at Austin College. David gave me and one of our guards, Don Ballard, a tour of the campus. We ate supper in the student cafeteria, played some ping pong, and then headed for a near-campus pool hall. Don and I were good pool players, and we started winning quite a few bucks. David just watched and rooted us on. The more we played, the better we got. We were so into the pool, we forgot about our 10 p.m. curfew. We noticed it was 10:25 p.m., and dropped our pool cues, and raced off for the dorm where we were staying. We were thirty-five minutes late. When we breathlessly arrived at our room, Coach Tilley was waiting for us, and he wasn't smiling. He told me I wouldn't play in the first two games and might not for the entire tournament. The question of my punishment wasn't up for debate. It didn't really matter to Don because he didn't play much anyway. He was better at pool than he was at basketball. I probably wasn't good enough for a big college scholarship anyway, but I was terribly embarrassed when I overheard Coach Tilley explaining to Austin College's head basketball coach, Chester Story, why I wasn't playing,

I feel confident I could have successfully snuck back in the dorm without Coach Tilley catching me were it not for unusual circumstances. The election of officers for our senior class had been held the day of our departure for Sherman. The ballots were counted that night, and our principal, Mr. Roark, upon learning that that two basketball players had won the presidency and vice-presidency of our senior class called Coach Tilley to give him the good news. Coach had gone to Guy Martin's room to give him the good news that he had been elected president and then came to my room to tell me I had been elected vice-president. I wasn't there, and it was after curfew. When I arrived, Coach Tilley asked me if I wanted the good news or the bad news first. Rats! But, my good friend Nancy was elected class secretary.

Sports in high school, like other major activities such as band, academics, music, drama, agriculture, etc., paid invaluable dividends to those who participated. They taught discipline to participants at a time in their lives it was most needed. They served as catalysts for the formation of friendships that would last lifetimes. They gave an added purpose and a sense of accomplishment to participants at a time when they were prone to self-doubt and insecurity. In my case, and despite my occasional game-costing goofs, sports gave me countless feel-good moments. They, also, boosted my confidence. I may have been the goat a few times, but I played. Glad I did. Memories of my high school sports moments – good and bad – pop in my head quite often I'm probably better in my memories than I was in real life, but so what?

High school memories are frequently firmly planted in our memory banks. They may lie dormant for decades, only to pop up when you least expect them. As you now know, I vividly remember the incident of me being thrown into the stands during a tussle in a basketball game in Lufkin. That may not be unusual, but I do find it noteworthy that one of the Lufkin students in the stands that night also remembered it long after it occurred. Let me explain.

Thirty-five years later, I was in Tokyo, Japan, on business. At the end of a long, hard day, I returned to my hotel and was walking to the front desk to retrieve my room key, when I heard a woman's voice say, "Excuse me, sir," in perfect English.

As I turned to see who she was talking to, I saw a woman waving rather frantically to me. She stood as I approached her, and she said she had an unusual question for me. She was well-dressed and rather attractive, so I said, "fire away." To my total shock and near disbelief, she asked me if I had played basketball for the Marshall Mavericks in 1964. When she saw the look of amazement on my face, she suggested we sit down for her explanation. It turns out she was a student in the bleachers in Lufkin the night of our fracas. Not only that, she was the pretty girl in whose lap my head had landed when I was thrown into the bleachers by her mob-like classmates. Her name was Lindia, and she was in Japan writing and photographing for a book she was publishing on Sumo wrestlers. What a memory she had, and we stayed in touch for a while after that Tokyo encounter.

Chapter 10

Bovine Diarrhea, and Stampeding Turkeys

It would have been awfully hard to grow up in Marshall, Texas, in the 1950s and '60s without coming into contact with farms, farmers, and farm animals. Marshall was surrounded by farms: tree farms, produce farms, grass farms, dairy farms, cattle farms (usually referred to as ranches, even if they were small), poultry farms, mink farms, rabbit farms, chinchilla farms, horse farms, honey farms, pig farms, and even worm farms.

I hadn't been directly exposed to many farms or farm families until I got to junior high and became friends with some farm kids. I had quite a few friends who lived in the country, but their families weren't really farmers. I suppose they just wanted to get away from the hustle and bustle of urban life represented by Marshall, although Marshall wasn't big enough to stir up much hustle or bustle. These folks usually had a few acres, a small barn, and a tractor with which to bush hog (mow) their land or, maybe, to put in a small garden. Quite often, this rural lifestyle also gave the man of the house an excuse to own a sweat-stained straw hat, a red bandana, a pair of blue overalls, and a pick-up truck. Down deep, it was in every East Texas man's DNA to want to own a pick-up truck. Maybe, sub-conscientiously, a fellow just feels a little manlier behind the wheel of a pick-up. Daddy once reminded me that most of his generation had been raised on farms and that these mini-farms provided many folks with a transition from farm life to city life. I know Daddy quietly wished for such a place, but it wasn't to be. At any rate, his logic made sense.

It seems to me that junior high and high school years had been set aside as learning years, book learning, for sure, but also social learning, boy-girl relationship learning, and world affairs learning. I, like most kids, raced through that period of my life, stacking up experiences at a rate far greater than my ability to process them. The sorting out of those experiences occurred slowly over the years. For some reason, many of my earliest learning experiences involved animals. I haven't a clue as to why that happened.

Once I got to junior high, Roy Lee Fry and I became good friends. Roy Lee lived out on Karnack Highway, and the Frys had a couple of acres of land behind their house where they kept a horse named Molly. I always thought it strange they named their horse Molly because one of Roy Lee's three sisters was also named Molly. I didn't spend much time fretting over this oddity, figuring if it didn't bother Sister Molly to have a horse with her name, it shouldn't bother me.

Roy Lee and I became very close and often slept over at each other's houses. One Saturday morning, after such a sleepover, Roy Lee suggested we saddle up Molly (the horse) and ride two miles down Highway 43 toward Karnack to a small grocery store he knew would sell cigars to two seventh-graders. I liked that plan because I was ready to try a cigar and because the trip would take us by the homes of two really cute girls, Linda Ratcliff and Martha Scott. I would have gladly forfeited the cigar for a chance visit with either Linda or Martha. Neither girl was in sight, but we found the store. We struggled with what kind of cigars to buy but narrowed our list of contenders to Swisher Sweets, rum-cured Crooks, or the fat Roi-Tans. We went with Swisher Sweets because Roy Lee said they smelled like cherries when lit.

I couldn't wait the get out of the store and light my Swisher Sweet. We walked around to the back of the store and lit up. Roy Lee was right; they did smell like cherries, but that's where the good news stopped. Instantly, I wondered how something could smell so good and, yet, taste so bad. I didn't let on to Roy Lee that I thought my Swisher Sweet tasted like Swisher Shit. I didn't want him to think I was uncool. Why a fellow could get the same taste sensation standing over a burning leaf pile and inhaling. Neither Roy Lee nor I could admit the cigar thing was a bad decision, so we kept puffing away as though they tasted great.

Our next move was to climb back aboard Molly and head home. Roy Lee told me he knew a backway to his house that would allow us to enjoy our Swisher Sweets away from the prying eyes of nosy adults. He headed Molly to the end of the store's driveway to a gate that lead into a large hayfield. I opened the gate and then re-latched it after we had passed through it, and we followed the fence line in the direction of home. Roy Lee said the field was part of a large farm owned by the Key Family and it ran along behind the homes that faced on Highway 43 so all we had to

Puberty Drove the Car

do was to follow the fence line to the back of the Ratcliff's property, exit at the gate, and we'd be home free. It was a lazy, hot East Texas day, and we had settled into the appropriate gait to match the day. Life was good, even if our Swisher Sweets weren't. Life was good for about 15 minutes, but then life got very complicated.

As we were ambling along, Roy Lee suddenly yelled for me to hold on and cranked Molly up to full gallop. I was holding on to Roy Lee with one arm and struggling to hang on to my Swisher Sweet with my free hand. As we bounced along, I could see the bright sun glistening through Roy Lee's blond crew cut. He was hunkered over like a jockey riding at Pimlico, and his new position made it hard for me to hold on. Molly's uneven gait caused my skinny little butt to bounce all over the place. My confusion over what caused this drastic interruption of our idyllic ride home cleared up the minute I saw a large horse running full speed at us with his masculinity standing at full attention. Roy Lee kept trying to coax more speed out of Molly in hopes of making it to the next exit gate before lover boy had his way with us. It was quickly evident we were gonna lose this race. Like a blur, this muscular, single-minded stud pulled up behind us. He was slinging his head from side to side, bucking, dancing, and snorting – all of which terrified me to no end. His flaring nostrils-added Tabasco to an already hot situation.

I may not have been the smartest boy in town, but I quickly surmised that if this highly-motivated stallion tried to consummate his love for Molly, I was going to be smushed by the weight of his upper body and carved up by his flailing forelegs. Roy Lee kept yelling at me to jump for the fence, get over it, and race down the fence line until I came to a gate. He wanted me to get the gate open for a hasty exit and then slam it shut to keep the stud at bay. His simple request was dang near impossible to accomplish. If I tried to jump for the fence, I would likely fall beneath the rampaging hooves of the horse from hell.

While I was trying to figure out how to get over the fence, the 1500 pound aroused stud reared behind Molly, and I got a close-up, disturbing glance at his underbelly, visual proof I had to get free from this passion drama right away. I also knew doing so would lighten Molly's load and allow her to speed up, so when one of Molly's kicks caught the stud in the chest and he momentarily backed off, I yelled for Roy Lee to get as close to the fence as possible. Once he got Molly next to the barbed wire, I bailed, throwing my body over the strung wire and catching the top strand with my left hand as the eager stud made his second attempt to mount Molly. Quickly to my feet, I tore out running down the fence row in search of a gate. Roy Lee spotted it first and spurred me on by telling me it was only about fifty more yards.

I hit my version of high gear while Roy Lee circled out into the field to buy me time to man the gate. Fortunately, there was no lock on the gate, and I was able to quickly unwind the chain that was secured to the fence post. When Roy Lee caught my signal, he headed for the gate as fast as Molly's kicking legs would carry them. Timing was everything, and mine and Roy Lee's were in perfect sync that day. I pulled the gate open enough for the fleeing Molly to slip through it and quickly slammed it shut before the still-horny stud could slip through. Roy Lee slid off Molly and ran over to re-fasten the chain while I was holding it shut. The spurned Romeo pranced back and forth in front of the gate, still squalling to the high heavens and stirring up dust. Roy Lee led Molly away from the fence and hid her from the stallion's sight. We then collapsed under a pine tree and tried to slow our runaway heart rates. Once the stallion lost sight of Molly, his breathing slowly returned to normal. With one last stomp and powerful head swing, he turned and slowly galloped off to wherever he had come from. The life-threatening drama was over. The drama was over, but not the trauma was not. It lingered.

As Roy Lee and I sprawled under the big pine, we began to reconstruct the events of the last few minutes that had brought us to this point. We wondered if Molly was "in season" and had emitted something into the air that aroused the stud. Or was she just a sexy, alluring horse that really turned on that particular steed and drove him to a state of unbridled desire? Or was the stud just so fired-up he would have pursued any mare with equal dedication? I'm fairly certain we didn't realize we had just encountered one of those "learning experiences" about which my dad was forever telling me.

I definitely learned some stuff from this equine romantic adventure. I learned that if you are on a mare that a horny stallion has taken a shine to, get off the mare. I learned that if you are just a kid and you decide to try a cigar, don't trust the smell of it and, that if you try it, do so with both feet planted firmly on the ground. Lastly, I learned that if you are riding double on a running horse, try not to be the second rider, or you will get some things crunched that you'd prefer went uncrunched.

My final two thoughts on this episode were that neither Roy Lee nor I remember what we did with our burning Swisher Sweets, and, that if you can envision a headline in your local newspaper that says, "Local

Youth Dies After Being Trampled by a Horny Stallion," you WILL find a way over a barbed-wire fence. By the way, the barbed wire cuts and scratches I sustained in my great escape eventually healed; an equine sexual encounter would not have. Thank you, Lord.

Another good friend I made in the seventh-grade was a red-headed country boy named Phil Parker. Phil's mother had been my fourth- grade teacher, so I had heard a lot about him before our paths finally crossed in Miss Estelle's English class. We hit it off quickly and soon were spending lots of time together. The Parkers had a large dairy farm west of town on Gum Springs Road. They lived in an antebellum two-story house that had large white columns in the front. When you threw in the large barns, corals, and stable, it made quite an impression on a boy who had grown-up in a nine-hundred square foot house in South Marshall. Even so, there was nothing haughty about the Parkers. Their home that was so stately from the outside had all the signs of being well lived in on the inside. There were piles of books on the formal dining table, dirty socks next to Mr. Parker's comfy chair in the den, and threadbare rugs in nearly every room. It was easy to relax at the Parker's. I felt at home.

My first overnight stay at Phil's was new and exciting. We rode his gray horse all over their farm, playing like the gullies and ravines were civil war trenches, and we were Confederates. We rode through the ravines, in and out of the trees, and over into their neighbor's forest land, giving rebel yells and air-stabbing Union soldiers with make-believe sabers. When we were fairly deep into the neighbor's land, Phil took on a different demeanor. He became very quiet, and we only walked his horse. Phil told me we had to be very careful we didn't jump a moonshine still. He said this part of rural East Texas was full of stills and that running up on one could cost you your life. The moonshiners lived in fear of being found by government revenuers and would defend their privacy at all costs. This fact was common knowledge to those of us who grew up in and around Marshall. Realizing we were entering the "danger zone," Phil re-directed his horse, getting us back to the safety of Parker land.

While we were out on horseback, Phil took me to a rocky half-acre where his family dumped all their garbage and trash. We weren't there to look at the mess. We were there to watch their goats munch away at any and all the trash. Until then, I didn't know goats ate tin cans. I was fascinated and could have watched those goats for hours.

Phil and I had enjoyed a busy day, and late that afternoon, we leaned against a fence and watched the dairy cows march single-file into the large milking barn for their last milking of the day. When the parade was over, Phil mixed up some sort of liquid feed and poured it into buckets, each of which had a large feeding nipple similar in appearance to a cow's teat. We each took a bucket into a small pen and let calves suck in their nourishment. The hungry calves attacked the nipples on the buckets with a ferocity that left me feeling a whole lot of sympathy for any mother cow with a suckling attached to her teat. We ran out of food for the buckets so Phil took them to a shed on the backside of the barn. While he was doing that, I decided to wander inside the large milking barn for a look at the cows, all of which were hooked up to the milking machines. Big, big mistake!

I very quickly learned that milk cows have an inherent fear – and I mean serious fear – of unfamiliar people, unfamiliar objects, unfamiliar situations, unfamiliar smells, unfamiliar noises, and sudden movements. As I walked in, I spotted Mr. Parker on the far side of the barn and, being the friendly boy I was, I hollered a loud greeting to him. I don't know if Mr. Parker heard me, but every cow in that barn did. They all turned their heads in my direction and quickly assessed me as being an unfamiliar person, an unfamiliar object, an unfamiliar smell, one who put them in an unfamiliar situation, a loud noise, and one who moves suddenly. Having made their assessment, all of them, in unison, began a frightful, non-stop bellow and, also in unison, dumped their bowels. I didn't know much about milk cows, but I knew a barn full of bawling, crapping, stomping, milk cows were not a good thing. My suspicions were confirmed when Mr. Parker ran over to me, grabbed me by the arm, and drug me out of the milk barn. Phil had returned from the shed, and, when I saw how big his eyes were as he took in the situation, I knew I wouldn't be getting a Christmas card from the Parkers. Mr. Parker glared at me and started to launch into a verbally-punishing lecture, but he stopped in mid-sentence and told Phil to get me away from the milk barn.

If I'd have had my way, I would have been staked-out on the Parker's trash pile so the goats could eat me. I don't remember what Phil and I did between that time and supper, but my mind couldn't rid itself of what I had just caused and witnessed. I simply had no idea milk cows were so fractious. Nor did I know their bowels held that much poop.

When Mrs. Parker rang the dinner bell, I truly dreaded sitting around the kitchen table with Phil, his older brother, Andy, and Mr. and Mrs. Parker. After a short blessing, we filled our plates, and conversation slowly started up. I just stared at my food, trying to ignore eye contact with any

Parker. It was Mrs. Parker who brought up the "incident" by saying, "Scotty, I understand you learned something about life on a dairy farm today."

I replied, "Yes, Ma'am," and kept stirring my mashed potatoes. Clearly, my giant mistake was about to become the topic of our dinnertime conversation. Mrs. Parker – ever the teacher – explained to me that dairy cows were totally creatures of habit and repetition, and when anything that altered their routine, particularly during milking, it frightened them so badly they went to pieces and got instant diarrhea. I wanted to tell her that that many squirting cows dang near gave this junior high boy diarrhea, too, but I didn't.

Mr. Parker must have taken a Valium before dinner because, in a very calm voice, he continued my education by telling me he milked his cows two or three times daily, and that each cow normally yielded fifty to seventy pounds of milk per day. He also told me each cow ate about one hundred pounds of grass or feed per day. Lastly, he told me that calm, relaxed cows gave up to twenty percent more milk than unhappy or frightened cows. After apologizing to Mr. Parker for the fiftieth time, I asked him if this incident would have a lasting effect on his herd. He just chuckled and told me it wouldn't and that the trauma only lasted about twenty minutes. I told him it would last a lot longer on me, and he told me to forget about it. As you can clearly see, the great milk cow melt-down occurred 60 years ago, and I learned a lot. For one, If you have something you don't know what to do with, give it to a goat. He'll eat it; and, if you are around milk cows, and one farts, run for the hills. The dam might be about to break!

We had a very good ninth-grade basketball team. We were called the Mighty Mites. We were kidded a bit by rival teams about being named for a tough mouse, but when you're winning, who cares? Our coach was Wade McNatt, and he was also head football coach of our Mighty Mites. Coach McNatt was in his late forties and, I guess, had probably risen as high as he was going to in the coaching ranks. Regardless of his future, we all liked Coach McNatt and enjoyed some of his idiosyncrasies. For example, he was very excitable and, when he was in a state of high excitement or anger, he was very animated, tending to butcher words and spray saliva when he was blasting out his wisdom or admonition. One always knew he was in for a verbal lashing when Coach got in your face and began with, "Dang, boy!"

I don't remember who we were playing, but one of our players had made mistake after mistake when he was on the court, and we were down at halftime. This player – who shall go unnamed for reasons that will become obvious – really was the primary reason we were trailing an inferior team. During the halftime break, Coach McNatt had us all sit down and launched into his review of our first-half performance. As usual, Guy Martin got well-deserved rave reviews. D. H. Martin and I got a few "well dones." Then, Coach stepped in front of our mistake-prone teammate, leaned over so that they were looking eye-to-eye, and said, "Dang, boy."

The tirade that followed was a stunner, and we couldn't believe what we were hearing. The besieged player, whom we shall call Simon, was a country boy who lived on the outskirts of town. The coach spat words in the face of Simon that went pretty much like the following:

> Dang, boy. You are playing the worst I've ever seen you play. You're costing us this game, and I need you to snap out of whatever funk you are in. You live out there on that farm, and I think you've been messing with the horses, the cows, the pigs, and the chickens, and I think it's sapping your strength! At this point, Simon had had all he could stand, and he jumped up, got right in Coach's grill, and hollered, I ain't ever messed with a chicken!

You could've heard a pin drop. Coach McNatt stood in stunned silence. The whole team stared slack-jawed at Simon and pondered what we had just heard. Had Simon just confessed to fooling around with horses, cows, and pigs? Our halftime pep talk appeared to have rolled all the way to the bottom of reality with a friend and teammate perhaps confessing to be a genuine animal lover. After a very awkward silence, during which Coach McNatt wiped the spittle off his chin, he half-heartedly clapped his hands and told us to go win the game.

Simon sat out the second half, and we won the game rather handily. It was a hollow victory, as all we could talk about was Simon's apparent confession. Given some thought, we decided Simon was innocent of his self-imposed charges and gave him the benefit of the doubt because he didn't even live on a farm. He lived just outside of Marshall and had neighbors on all sides. His family had no horses, cows, pigs, chickens, or sheep, for that matter. We felt as though Simon needed to listen to Coach more carefully in the future, lest he only get part of the message and respond with a poorly thought-out answer.

There were, of course, lingering questions. For example, was there a farm near Simon's house that had a barnyard full of animals that were the objects of his desire? Did Simon have a deep-seated chicken phobia that prompted this outburst of denial when Coach mentioned chickens? I ran around quite a bit with Simon throughout our high school years, and I never noticed even the slightest of animal fondness on his part. He ended up dating some really cute girls, so either his tastes had improved, or the chicken faux pas was just an anomaly. We'll never know for sure, but I'll die believing Simon just went through a stupid moment during that halftime encounter with Coach McNatt.

I can't say I learned a whole lot from this particular "learning experience." Well, maybe I learned that we should choose our words very, very carefully before we blurt out an emotional response to any question. Right, Simon?

As I got into high school and became a legal driver (I was driving long before I had my license), more and more of my "learning experiences" involved girls. Some of those stories I won't share with you. Some of them I can't share with you. Here's one I can and will share with you. However, let me point out that after fifty-three blissful years of marriage, I still have daily "learning experiences" about girls.

There were gorgeous girls everywhere I looked in high school, but some were more gorgeous than others. One girl I thought was a real stunner was Becky Shoults. Now, I realize someone who's gorgeous to one boy may not be gorgeous to another boy, but, to my way of thinking, a boy would have had to be as crazy as a peach orchard boar to leave Becky off his list. I wasn't crazy, and I was thrilled one night when Becky and I had a chance to get better acquainted down at our local hangout, Neely's on Grand. We chatted and laughed for quite some time, and when it was time to head home, Becky agreed to let me drive her home. The Shoults family lived out on Harleton Highway, a few miles northwest of Marshall, on a large turkey farm that bore their name. Shoults turkeys and the family's company, Bear Creek Farms, were well-known throughout much of the country. I knew nothing about turkeys, but I knew of Shoults turkeys. More importantly, I had a crush on Becky Shoults and, at that moment, I was living the dream.

As I pulled in the Shoults' driveway, I saw the family home perched on a hill, overlooking much of their acreage as well as their company's offices, which were off to one side. The paved area around the offices provided guest parking, and that's where I parked my 1955 Ford. It was a beautifully moonlit night, so Becky and I exited the car and leaned against it, just enjoying the great evening. Really, I think we were just stalling, trying to work up the nerve to do some hugging and smooching. She was even prettier in moonlight. I may – and I stress, may – have kissed Becky on the cheek. If I didn't, it wasn't from a lack of desire, just a case of shyness. We decided there was enough moonlight to allow us to walk to a hill that was behind their house. As we neared the hill, I spotted a flatbed trailer that had a few bales of hay on it and a liberal amount of loose hay strewn around on its surface. We decided to climb up on the trailer, lean against the hay bales, enjoy the moonlight, and cuddle some. The hugging led to some kissing – nothing heavy, but enough to excite me and cause me to jump to my feet and give a thunderous Tarzan yell as an expression of my total joy. Oh, brother, was that ever the wrong thing to do – a horribly wrong thing to do.

You may recall from history classes that Ben Franklin wanted the turkey to be named our national bird. He was quoted as saying, "Turkeys are birds of courage." Well, let me tell you, Old Ben never met the Shoults' turkeys. They were anything but courageous, and when startled by my ill-advised Tarzan yell, they went into full-fledged gobble mode and took off running at full speed in all directions. Yours truly had started an all-out turkey stampede of epic proportions. A shoulder-to-shoulder army of rampaging birds stormed by us, frantically trying to get to God only knew where. Soon after the gobbling and race to nowhere started, Mr. Shoults woke up and turned on enough outside floodlights to light Cowboy Stadium to see just what set his turkeys off. I'm certain he thought a pack of wolves or coyotes had attacked his massive flock – more correctly referred to as a rafter, by the way. He stepped out of his back door with his shotgun cradled in his arms. Little did he know – at least at that point – that the problem he was witnessing with his turkeys had been started by the very biggest turkey on his farm that night, yours truly.

Becky had fear stamped all over her lovely face. She stood with her fingers across her lips as she watched the feathered bedlam run aimlessly to and fro before our very eyes. Finally, she looked at me and calmly told me that turkeys are very skittish and panic when startled. Really? I had news for her. Marshall High school boys panic, too, when they cause thousands of turkeys to panic, and the man who owns the turkeys is walking toward him with a shotgun in his arms. Becky caught the attention of her dad, Hick Shoults, as he (and his shotgun) were walking toward us. I was off the hay wagon, trying desperately to look like a boy who had never kissed a girl in his entire life. If I could have, I would have joined the running turkeys and not stopped until I got to Oklahoma. The last thing on earth I wanted to do was stand toe-to-toe with an angry man holding a 12-gauge pump shotgun.

Becky ran to her dad and stopped him about twenty feet before he reached me. She was talking ninety miles an hour, and, as he listened to her, he kept glancing over her shoulder at me. At the end of their chat, they walked over to me, and Mr. Shoults introduced himself, and we shook hands. He was a man of few words, which was fine with me. He then walked off to do whatever turkey magnates do when their livelihoods race off over the hill, screaming the whole way. After apologizing profusely to Becky for stampeding the family's birds, I sheepishly crawled into my Ford and headed home. Becky and I saw each other several more times, but we didn't hang around the turkey farm on those occasions.

When I told this story to my Uncle Curly, he asked me if I knew how many turkeys were killed in the stampede. After seeing the shocked and confused look on my face, he told me all about domesticated turkeys and their vast differences from their wild brethren. Curly knew about such things and gave me a lesson in turkeys. Apparently, turkeys in the wild are quite intelligent and very resourceful. They can run up to twenty-five miles per hour and fly about the same speed. Curly said Ben Franklin was right in citing the intelligence and courage of wild turkeys.

On the other hand, turkeys raised in captivity share very few of those traits and do not develop survival skills. Since they are raised to be fat and meaty, they can't run quickly and are clumsy on their feet. They can't fly at all because their wings are clipped at an early age. In short, they are basically dumb and helpless. When frightened, they will run until they encounter a barrier, often stacking up at that barrier and trampling other turkeys to death or suffocating those at the bottom of the heap. An interesting tidbit my learned uncle told me was that male turkeys – toms – all have a flap of flesh that hangs over their beak called a snood. Turkey hens decide which tom to mate with based on the length of his snood. Hmm. Don't believe it when someone tells you size doesn't matter.

Even today, I haven't the foggiest idea of how many turkeys died because of my exuberance expressed through a Tarzan yell. I never had the nerve to ask Becky, and I never returned to Shoults Turkey Farms for fear I would run into her dad. Perhaps as a self-imposed penance, I have bought many, many Shoults turkeys to put on our Thanksgiving dinner tables or to give as gifts to family and friends.

For weeks after my embarrassing encounter with a vast flock of nervous, quick-to-panic turkeys, I kept flashing back to the devastating experience and to the one I had gone through with the Parker's milk cows. Those massive humiliations made me think, or perhaps realize I would make a lousy farmer. I seemed to have a toxic effect on farm animals, especially the jumpy ones.

If my junior and senior high school years were designed to be learning years, I was right on script. The stampeding turkeys incident was just one more example of the unusual ways learning sneaks up on you. It taught me lots of things and helped me make some decisions about the future. I decided that if Becky and I ever saw each other again, it would be in town, not at Shoults Turkey Farm. I decided the only turkeys I like are those served on a platter during holiday meals. Lastly, I learned that if you are ever on any kind of farm and enjoy a wonderful kiss from a pretty girl, you should keep your elation to yourself. You never know who or what might hear your joyful yell. It might even be something that poops uncontrollably or stampedes into the next county while gobbling the whole way. Neither event is productive or fun to watch.

When I was a small boy growing up in rural Texas, it was commonplace for Daddy to teach my brothers and me what kind of cows, horses, chickens, pigs, etc. we saw through our car windows as we rode through the countryside. Uncle Curly did the same thing. We all learned to identify the different breeds on sight. It made our trips fun, and it taught us an appreciation for farms, ranches, and the animals on them. I still play that game with myself when on car trips. My wife, Kay, discourages my doing so because she, rightfully, says it distracts me from my driving.

However, the memories of the events I've shared with you in this chapter still burn brightly in me. I am still affected by those events. For example, when I see two boys up on the back of a horse taking a slow walk at the highway's edge, I instinctively glance around to make certain there is no super-inspired stallion heading their way with lovin' on his mind. Anytime I see a dairy farm or a field full of milk cows, I reach over and turn my radio down on the odd chance I could cause massive diarrhea. Just seeing a milking barn floods my olfactory senses with the smell of cow poop. That impression will never die in me. What happens when I see a turkey farm? I don't know. I can't recall seeing one since the night of the stampede. I tend to think my negative thoughts would be chased away by the memory of Becky's kiss. I really like the farm animals. My favorites? Mules, hands down.

Chapter 11

Friends: Old and New

Leaving South Marshall Elementary School and entering Marshall Junior High School would have been a near traumatic experience for me had I not been making that transition in the company of all my friends from South Marshall. I felt a deep and personal tie to those kids with whom I had gone to school for six years. I still do.

In *Mad Dogs, Marbles, and Rock Fights*, I wrote of my early years from pre-school through the sixth grade. More importantly, I wrote about the shenanigans my friends and I pulled along the way. I profiled each of my closest friends. They were: Terry Weeks, Charlie Starke, David Applebaum, Clarence Warnstaff, David Reeves, Tuck Kemper, Dick Cole, Frank Timmins, and David Wist. All of those friends except David Reeves and Dick Cole would be starting junior high with me. David moved to Dallas, and Dick, who was three years older than me, would be starting high school. Over time, some of those friends may have drifted a little from me, but I didn't drift away from any of them. Even today, they are still part of my core group of friends. All this blubbering aside, the point I'm trying to make is that any venture into the unknown is best made in the company of friends.

What I underestimated about junior and senior high school was the number of new friends that would cause me to expand the tight little circle of my close friends. In junior high, Phil Parker, Roy Lee Fry, Mike Briggs, John Bogue, Mickey McCay, Glenn Thomas, Will DuShane, and Ronnie McMullen became good buddies.

Longtime buddy Terry Weeks in his driveway

 I quickly decided that one of junior high's positive aspects was that it dumped me into a larger pool of individuals, many of whom I thought to be great kids. Now, to be fair, that larger pool of kids also exposed me to several kids who weren't so great. But, what the heck? I figured it was worth putting up with a lot of crap if you could come out of the tedium with a handful of great friends.

John Bogue looking cool in his flat top

John, Mickey, and Will gained entrance into the core group of friends who earned permanent places in a corner of my heart reserved for the closest of the close.

John and I met through junior high football and basketball. I'll not complicate this description of John with an amateurish analysis or needless platitudes. John never embraced pretension of any sort. He reeked of honesty, loyalty, trustworthiness, and strength of character.

My dad agreed with my assessment and, in my book, that was a hell of a fine endorsement of my friend, John. He has gone through life carrying a load of goodness everywhere he's gone. Oh, John wasn't perfect, but his imperfections were – and are – harmless. On those rare occasions when John crossed the line of impropriety, I was usually the one who led him astray. John and I are both in our seventies now, but we are still very, very close. As an aside, when John found out I would be writing this memoir that talked about our high school years, he put me on notice that if I told all of our shared secrets and adventures, I would be hearing from his attorney. Don't worry, John. I would never throw you under the bus, for, if I did, I would be pulled under with you.

I must tell one story on John, or, more accurately, how John put one over on some of his friends. One hot afternoon, we were all bored and stumped as to what to do to break the boredom. John then told us he knew a secluded field off of Highway 43 just covered with the sweetest watermelons in East Texas, just lying there for the taking. We all perked up and jumped in John's Studebaker Lark and lost ourselves in anticipation of the melon trove we were about to invade. John knew what he was talking about. He drove us down several winding dirt roads until he pulled next to a barbed-wire fence that stood sentry around the best-looking field of ripe melons I had ever seen. Before we started our poaching, John warned us that the old man who owned this field of melons was a grumpy old farmer who would shoot us full of buckshot if he caught us stealing his Black Diamonds. He told us we had to be fast, alert, and quiet. Operation "melon snatch" got off to a good start, and we had piled up about six big melons next to John's car. As we cleared the fence to get more melons, John yelled for us to get back in the car now, because the old man was topping the hill in his pick-up truck and heading right for us. Before we could get out of there, the old man pulled up and parked behind John's car, exited his truck, and walked briskly up to John's window. He then bent over and glared in at Terry, Mickey, and me and opened John's door. With huge eyes that conveyed fear, John looked at us as if to say, "we've had the green weenie now." He then crawled out of the car, and as we were about to write John off, he and the old man hugged. John then leaned in his window with a huge smile on his face and told us to get out and meet his granddaddy. John had pulled a good one over on us. Plus, his granddaddy let us keep the melons.

I had met Mickey in summer league baseball, but we became great friends by sharing the backfield on our junior high football team. Mickey was our right halfback, and I was our left halfback. He ran up the middle. I ran to the outside. Mickey was one of five children and was used to sharing. He didn't have a stingy bone in his body or a devious thought in his brain. Mickey was an open book with simple goodness oozing off of each page. If he wasn't laughing, he was close to doing so. He, like John, was honest and loyal. Now, before I paint Mickey as a Johnny Appleseed sort of fellow skipping through life sowing seeds of good cheer, let me assure you Mickey could be pushed into action. For example, his high school sweetheart was Diane Morris. Mickey found out "Pudge" Hortman was trying to woo Diane into a date, and it didn't sit well with Mickey at all. That night, Mickey pulled into the Dairy Queen on Grand where Hortman was parked, got out of his car, calmly walked over to Pudge's car, and signaled for him to roll down his window. When Pudge complied, Mickey launched a hard right that caught Pudge square on the jaw. Mickey waited a second to see if the now woozy Pudge wanted to exit the car to continue their "discussion." Pudge just rolled his window back up, cranked up, and left. Mickey returned to his car. Pudge never said another word to Diane. My friend Mickey died unexpectedly in his fifties. I think of him daily and truly miss his goodness.

Now, Will was happy. Or, if he wasn't, he was a master at keeping it to himself. The only time Will wasn't smiling was when he was laughing. Will, like John and Mickey, was totally unpretentious and of solid gold character. There was never a hidden agenda with Will. The two of us went through junior high, high school and college together, and not one single time did I ever question the strength of his character or forthrightness. Will was refreshingly true. I always admired Will.

I did manage to get Will mad at me one time in college. Will lived in a men's dorm called the Units. The Units were three long single story buildings built motel style. Terry Weeks and I also shared a room in the Units about eight rooms down from Will's. Will worked his way through college as a pizza delivery man. His job often kept him out long hours, so when he did get to his room, he usually quickly dropped into a deep sleep. On one of those "deep sleep" nights, Terry and I decided to pull a prank on Will. We snuck up to Will's dorm window and verified he was in his bed, which was next to the window. We then squirted lighter fluid under his door and onto his tile floor. Next, we lit the lighter fluid and banged loudly on his door. He was supposed to wake up to see the flames leaping up at the foot of his bed. We stood by to watch his reaction. We kept standing by. No reaction. When we peered in the window again, we saw that Will was still asleep and, horror of horrors, his bed covers had caught on fire! We began pounding on his door and window, screaming for him to wake up. His room was filling with smoke, and the flames from his fire-consumed covers were about to engulf Will, yet he kept sawing logs. Just before we broke out his window, he roused up and sprang into action. He threw his door open and heaved his flaming covers onto the sidewalk.

When he spotted Terry and me standing there holding a can of Ronson lighter fluid, he quickly figured out the drama that had just played out. Will wounded us with his eyes, scorched us with his tongue, and shooed us back to our rooms before he committed justifiable homicide. I doubt Will ever completely forgave us for our prank-gone-bad, but he did allow us back into his good graces. I hope I'm still there. As close as I've always felt to Will, I believe there is much about him I will never know. He simply never shared his past or his inner most thoughts. I never needed to know everything about him to know he was my dear friend.

As I entered high school, I became closer to Dickie Brassell, Jim Elliott, Butch Kennedy, Reeves Field, and Johnny Galik. I also added a friend named Jimmy Faucett. Jimmy, whom we called "Leaky," was a very, very slow-talking fellow, even by East Texas standards. His movements matched his pace of talking and, unless he was motivated to action, his sloth-like actions could darn near put one in a catatonic state. We often played tackle football after school, with full non-uniformed teams going at it hard. Jimmy shined in those games. He ran like the wind and, sometimes, ran you over just for the fun of it. He had "fast" in him, for sure. He just didn't waste it on talking and walking. Leaky lived right down Merritt Street from me. Merritt was only about three and one-half blocks long, but Leaky and I were joined on it by John and Jimmy.

My Pal Dick Brassell Leaning Against His Red Corvair

Leaky graduated a year ahead of me and took off for Texas A & I College in Kingsville, Texas (now Texas A&M-Kingsville). Kingsville was way down in South Texas, 452 miles from Marshall. When I asked Jimmy why he chose to go to school there, he said, "I don't know. Never been there." When Jimmy came home for the first time after going to Kingsville, he told me he was on the college rodeo team. I was shocked because, to my knowledge, Jimmy had ridden very few horses in his day and knew nothing about livestock. I nearly fainted when he said he made the team as a bull rider. I knew rodeoing was bigger in Kingsville than football was. After all, it was home to the modest little 825,000-acre King Ranch. Kingsville was cowboy central for Texas, if not the world. How did my friend, Jimmy "Leaky" Faucett, end up being a bull-riding cowboy? When I asked him to explain it all to me, he boiled it down to two things. Firstly, he said the cowboys got all the girls, and, secondly, he confessed he was not a very good bull rider and that I shouldn't be overly impressed. Faucett logic didn't always make sense to me, but no matter. Jimmy either tired of the South Texas girls or tired of getting his ass busted by angry bulls because he left Texas A & I and Kingsville after a semester or two. He then joined his dad and brother Harold as welders on the pipeline. Jimmy and I slowly lost track of each other, but he's still my friend, and I would love to see him again and catch that possum-eating-persimmons grin of his. Where are you, Leaky?

Chapter 12

Mrs. Jones Had an Affair with A Fairy

I am willing to bet anyone that he or she – regardless of their age – holds a number of their teachers in a special place in their heart and credits them with having had a very positive influence on their life. I certainly do. I am, also, willing to bet anyone that he or she had a few teachers that were so wacky and/or different that they are permanently engraved on their memory because of their oddity. I certainly did.

I had never been afraid of a teacher…until the seventh-grade. That's when I encountered a junior high science and history teacher named Robert Bacher. Even though I never had Mr. Bacher for a class, he went on my "watch list" when I saw him break up a fight between Pete George and some other kid. He didn't just separate the two warriors; he joined the scuffle and single-handedly physically subdued both guys at the same time. This feat was not an easy one to pull off because both boys were as tough as nails and as wild as two bobcats with nicotine under their tails. When the fight was over and Mr. Bacher dragged the combatants off to the principal's office, those of us who had witnessed the fight were abuzz about how efficiently and firmly this teacher had restored order. We all agreed that Mr. Bacher really knew how to handle himself and that he was not a man to roil.

The next time I witnessed Mr. Bacher in action was during a duck-and-cover drill that filled the hallways with kids practicing how to escape death in the event of tornados or atomic bombs. Apparently, Scooter Newton had created a moment of levity during the drill that caused several students to laugh uncontrollably. Scooter had farted. Mr. Bacher quickly figured out the source of the disruption, grabbed

Scooter by the shoulders, and rammed his head into the nearest locker door with considerable force. Mr. Bacher was a man who believed rules were to be followed and was willing to act to enforce them. Mr. Bacher's reputation for keeping order spread throughout the school. Word, also, soon spread that he had seen lots of action in the Pacific during World War II, and more action in the Korean War, and that he came home from both wars with numerous medals for valor. I do not know if those rumors were true or if they were part of the lore students often invented about their teachers. I do know his students really liked him (except for Scooter Newton). I also know he doted on his five children, and the Bachers were faithful attendees at the First Baptist Church of Marshall. While I kind of feared Mr. Bacher, I think he was a teacher who provided a strong role model for lots of boys. Even today, I think it's fine for students to have a little fear of their teachers and the power they have.

There were several teachers, usually women, who were soft on misconduct, a fact that lead to their being abused by rowdy junior high boys. Reluctantly, I now admit I was among those students who made life a living hell for some of those "fragile" teachers. Personally, I deeply regret the way I treated Miss Elizabeth Orr, my eighth-grade English teacher. If she was alive today, I would seek her out and offer her my most sincere apologies. I would apologize, but then I would tell her what had caused her male students to treat her with such disrespect. I would tell her she should have corrected us without getting in our faces and screaming at us. I would tell her she should not have treated each rule infraction as though it was an Alcatraz-worthy crime, always earning the offender a trip to the principal's office. Our principal, Miss Emma Mae Brotze, was a hardline disciplinarian, but she was sick and tired of putting out grass fires set by our match-happy English teacher.

Once, Miss Ohr hauled me to the principal's office and was so mad at me that she was yelling and slobbering in front of all who were present in the office. Miss Emma Mae Brotze rolled her eyes as if to say, "here we go again," and calmly escorted us across the hall into the empty auditorium where she could arbitrate in a quiet environment. She sat between Miss Ohr and me and started by asking the prosecutor, Miss Ohr, to present her case as to why I should be executed. She listened carefully to Miss Ohr, thanked her, and asked me to give my version of the events that led to this confrontation. After

I had done so, Miss Brotze paused thoughtfully and then told Miss Ohr she had vastly overreacted. Miss Brotze then told Miss Ohr she MUST learn to control her rage. She then shooed both of us back to class. We walked back upstairs to our classroom without ever saying a word to each other.

Given the chance, I would also tell her that, if she had moved her plants away from the window sill, Tucker Conley wouldn't have been able to push them out of the second story window onto the sidewalk below that ran in front of the band hall. The last thing I would tell her would be that the blue dress she so often wore to school looked nice on her, but she could have tightened the belt about four or five notches. She always wore the matching blue belt far too loose, and it looked comical. It made it hard for us to take her seriously as our instructor. It wasn't fashionable to wear saggy belts at that time. It was just stupid. Who knows? Maybe a tight belt gave her gas or irritated an old belly scar.

In fairness to Miss Ohr, there were several nasty tricks played on her that kept her off balance. We were required to use real ink fountain pens in English and, in support of this requirement, each English class kept a very large bottle of Scripto blue ink near the front of the class for communal use. Students were free to fill their pens at will. It was common practice for some of the boys to fill their pens and then squirt their contents onto Miss Ohr's prize plants. I never saw any of her plants turn blue, but the ink couldn't have been good for them. Some students had pens with ink cartridges in them. When their cartridges ran dry, they would use the hypodermic needle that stayed next to the big ink bottle to suck ink into it, which, in turn, would be used to inject ink into their empty cartridge. Paul Wood and David Wist would bring small bottles of saltwater from home, fill the hypodermic with it, and then inject Miss Ohr's ivy with salt water. The ivy died, and its death – over and over – kept her in a botanical fog. Oh, dear, Miss Ohr, I am so sorry. Paul and David clearly deserved a trip to the office!

Speaking of Paul and David, they, along with a few others, were tough on one of our elderly teachers, a kindly old gal named Wilma Attebery. Mrs. Attebery was deaf as a board and found little relief from her hearing aid. She split her time between teaching history and minding the library. Paul, David, and their compadres had study hall under Mrs. Attebery and quickly learned that if they hummed in unison when the hearing-challenged teacher walked by, she would assume her hearing aid was acting up. She would remove it, shake it, and sometimes pound it on the desk, trying to rid it of the annoying hum. If she ever caught on to their cruel trick, it was after they had moved on to the next grade.

A quick story about how punishing students could be to teachers who showed their vulnerabilities involved my good friend, Tuck Kemper. Tuck had a music appreciation class, which was mandatory for seventh-graders, taught by Miss Kyle. Miss Kyle was young, unsure of herself, jittery, and always appeared as though she was ready to burst into tears. She had a tough time maintaining order in her room, which signaled the class disruptors to pour it on. One day, after a test, Miss Kyle instructed the students to pass their papers to the left, where she could easily collect them. Leonard a.k.a "Pudgy," sat on Tuck's left. Tuck passed his paper to Leonard, who added a horizontal mark through the "T" in Tuck's name. As Miss Kyle collected the papers, she noticed the "nastification" of Tuck's name and turned red as a beet. It was clear to all that a flustration bomb had detonated inside the shy, and perhaps naïve, young teacher. She seemed stymied by the transition of Tuck's name. Finally, she took Tuck out to the hall and read him the riot act. Today, Tuck still doesn't know if she bought the story about Leonard being the one who went obscene on his name. From that day forward, Tuck never signed anything "Tuck" again. He now signs everything "Thomas Kemper." Miss Kyle may have forgotten the embarrassing incident over the years, but my buddy, Tuck, never has.

Hands down, the weirdest teacher I ever had at any grade or level was Mrs. Maugherite (yes, that's the way she spelled it) Jones. Mrs. Jones was my ninth-grade English teacher. I loved her immensely and learned volumes from her. I suppose she was in her sixties when she taught me, but she could have easily passed for 160. Regardless of her age, she was filled with boundless energy and excitement for her craft. She was a very small lady who looked as though she had just crawled out of a laundromat dryer. Wrinkles owned her face as well as her clothes. Her freckles and age spots added to her unkempt look, and her wild eyes seemed like they had just seen something unbelievable. Her hair always featured a tuft that went rogue on her and took a left when it should've gone right. Her lipstick looked as though something had startled her badly as she was putting it on, causing it to stray widely from her lip lines. She always gave me the impression she was about to fly off into a land no one else had ever visited. One day every week, all year long, Mrs. Jones wore a white blouse that had a huge tear down its backside. We all used to wonder why she didn't throw it away, or, at least, sew it up. I still don't understand her loyalty to that rag of a blouse. Perhaps she never noticed it was torn. The torn blouse, the smeared lipstick, and the irreverent hair became symbols of Mrs. Jones's quirkyness.

Mrs. Jones taught us classic literature, such as *Ivanhoe* and *Beowulf*. She not only taught us these classics, she brought them to life by having us act them out. She walked among us as she taught, frequently involving us in the discussion. We had to pay attention for fear she would ask for our input. She enthralled us with the story of *Beowulf* and, believe me, that takes some teaching. She was an entertaining, effective teacher who proved to me that learning could be fun.

Mrs. Jones's real literary love was Shakespeare and, boy, could she teach it. She reached us kids, and we left her class at the end of the year with a keen appreciation for the genius of Shakespeare and a working knowledge of plays such as *Othello*, *The Tempest*, *Twelfth Night*, *The Taming of the Shrew*, and her favorite, *A Midsummer Night's Dream*.

One got to experience Mrs. Jones in her full glory when she taught us *A Midsummer Night's Dream*. It wasn't just her enthusiasm and animation that brought this play to life, it was that she was assisted in her teaching effort by one who had the inside scoop on the play. He joined us every day in class, and he and Mrs. Jones co-taught us through their constant exchange of dialogues and ideas. Oh, oh. At this point, I should tell you her teaching assistant was none other than Puck, the fairy that was Oberon's jester in the play itself. As she was teaching, Mrs. Jones would sometimes stop, stare at the imaginary Puck, and ask him a question about the play. After an appropriate amount of time, she would thank Puck and tell us what the fairy had told her. She would even stop mid-sentence on occasion to allow Puck to interject some thought he had that might help us understand some part of the play better. Puck was so real to her – at least in the drama she was unfolding in front of us – that she would sometimes stop a student from sitting in his or her seat because Puck was sitting there. The bewildered student would have to stand until Puck changed locations. One time, Tommy Banks was made to stand in the hallway for more than half a class because he had sat on Puck. Dang, Tommy. Watch where you sit! She was very unhappy with Tommy.

We all learned to enjoy Puck's presence in our class, and we listened intently to Puck's messages as they were relayed to us by Mrs. Jones. She often professed her love for Puck. Many of Mrs. Jones' students felt as though she truly believed in Puck and truly believed he was present in her classroom. They also believed she really was in love with the little fairy. Was she totally nuts, or was she the most creative teacher of her generation? I don't know for sure, but I also don't care. She was a teaching genius in my mind. Mrs. Jones has been gone a long time now, but whenever I think of that wild-eyed, disheveled little lady, I now envision her sitting in a remote, shady spot, carrying on an enlivened discussion about literature with her long-time "lover," Puck. And, oh yes, she's still wearing that torn white blouse.

Junior high was over for us with the end of our ninth-grade year. Our attention then turned to speculating on our ascension to Marshall Senior High School and what it would be like. We had just completed a year of being the big shots in junior high, and now we were, once again, spiraling down to being lowly sophomores, the lowest rung on the high school social ladder. We were still super excited. The high school girls were women. Car-dating, dances, high school sports, the ability to get jobs (and, therefore, money), were just a few of the things that fueled our anticipation. We had heard many things about high school, including the straight skinny on which teachers were good, which were bad, which were easy A's, which were very hard, etc. I'll now talk about a few of those teachers that earned their mention in this chapter.

A few of our teachers had become somewhat legendary by the time I reached high school. For instance, there were two rather old sisters named Sydney and Berta Akin who lived together on a farm where they raised produce when they weren't teaching. Neither sister ever married. It was common knowledge that both ladies were expert marksmen and that with a .22 rifle in hand, either one could split a pecan in half when it was thrown into the air. Now, for city folks who may struggle to relate to such a feat, let me tell you, that is some very fine shooting. That neat little trick would have earned those ladies jobs in Buffalo Bill's Wild West show right alongside Annie Oakley. While I never had either sister for a class, I always looked at them with unbridled admiration for their shooting prowess. I asked Miss Sidney if the rumors about the pecan-splitting accuracy of her shooting were true. She looked me square in the eyes and said, "yes." 'Nuff said. The Akin sisters never had to worry about me and my buddies stealing watermelons from their field. No way.

Inez Hughes was an English teacher with a reputation as a fine teacher, a tough disciplinarian, and a teacher who left no room for short-cuts. She carried herself like a Marine Corps drill instructor and physically conveyed a no-nonsense attitude. One time, Mrs. Hughes, who was either a widow or divorced, insisted Phil Parker and I accompany her to a live operatic production of Verdi's *La Traviata*. We were reluctant attendees and, as we feared, it was torture to both of us. Mrs. Hughes sat between us, but Phil and I managed to record our disdain for the evening with each other through the exchange of eye frowns. On the way home from the opera, Mrs. Hughes asked us what we thought of the arias. Phil took me off the hook by answering, "I thought the auditorium was a little hot." She didn't even respond.

Mrs. Hughes was big on having students stand before the class to give oral book reports. When a student tried to give an abbreviated report or tried to con her, Mrs. Hughes would drill the reporter with complex questions designed to ferret out whether the kid had actually read the book. She had no qualms about nailing a student in front of the entire class. I remember one student who obviously suffered from jock itch. He kept his left hand in his Levi's pocket, where it was fully-engaged in scratching his infected area all the time he was giving his report. His maneuver was distractingly obvious to everyone in the class, including Mrs. Hughes. When she had tolerated the talk and scratch report as long as she could, she blurted out for him to stop talking and to stop scratching. She told him he could finish his report after he had cured the malady that afflicted him. His public scratch-fest earned him the nickname "Scratch," a moniker that stuck with him through his remaining high school years and maybe even into college where he graduated as a doctor of dentistry.

In summing up my experiences with Mrs. Hughes, I learned a lot from her. I also think that by doing things such as exposing Phil and me to something as alien to our backgrounds as opera, she helped round out a couple of rough-edged boys in whom she saw promise. I suppose there are still teachers who go that extra mile in teaching by extending education beyond the three o'clock bell. I hope so, because it pays off. I will say, in all honesty, that trip to see *La Traviata* was largely wasted on me. I can't stand opera, and Phil was right. It was sort of a little hot in that auditorium.

The last teacher I want to talk about was a book unto herself. Her name was Miss Selma Brotze. She was the English-teaching sister of my junior high principal, Miss Emma Mae Brotze. She was also one of the people to whom I dedicated my earlier book, *Mad Dogs, Marbles, and Rock Fights*. Miss Selma was a piece of work and, while I am tempted to do her biography right here, I will confine my remarks to a few of the characteristics and actions that made her the most-respected teacher in Marshal for fifty years.

If I had to pick one word that represented the core of her teaching, it would be "creativity." Her desire was to teach young minds to lift the lids off their imaginations, thereby enabling them to revel in the joy that comes from freeing themselves from the mundane and learning to think and act creatively. I was not the kind of student who could easily find "X" in an algebraic problem, but I was the kind of student who could easily unleash my creative side and see things in multi-colors versus just black and white. Finally, I had found a teacher who asked me to see, sense, hear, and smell the forest, not just see a single tree. I loved her style, and we hit it off very well, very fast.

Miss Selma was odd enough to always be interesting. She bummed a cigarette from David Wist one time after class. We all knew she smoked Lucky Strikes and, at that time, so did David. It was somewhat scandalous for women to smoke in public back then, particularly if she was a teacher. If some poor kid forgot his or her deodorant one day, Miss Selma would go stand by that student and announce in an exaggerated theatrical style, "Lord, child, someone forgot their deodorant today." She would then fan with her hand and go to the nearest classroom window and shove it open to let in fresh air. Many girls, particularly my friend Judy Ford, were intimidated by the unbridled Miss Selma and lived in fear of being called on by her. It was painfully clear she favored boy students over girl students, and she would seat her favorite students on the front row, nearest to her desk. Wist and I had been seated right across from her desk. She clearly liked us a lot, but she might also have wanted us where she could keep an eye on us.

If Sleepy had ever resigned from the Seven Dwarfs, David Wist would have been a natural replacement. David could not stay awake in class. He couldn't stay awake riding around in a car. He couldn't stay awake at your house if he came over for a visit. His mother thought he was just lazy. His teachers thought he probably had a bad home life and didn't get enough sleep. Doctors told his parents not to worry, that he was probably just going through a growth spurt. Everyone – including the teachers – knew he was one of the smartest kids in high school, but his sleepiness was legendary. David and I sat next to each other, and Miss Selma told me to keep David awake as much as I could. I let him catnap when she was patrolling the back of the room and roused him up when she headed for the front. Years later, David was diagnosed as having been a long-suffering narcoleptic. Yawn. You didn't miss much, David.

As I said, Miss Selma played favorites. Our senior year, I was one of 30 students assigned to her for homeroom. To kick the year off, the first order of business was for each homeroom to elect a president, a vice-president, and a secretary. Roy Lee and I were nominated for president, and Miss Selma had us go out into the hallway while the class voted. We were then brought back in, and Miss Selma announced that I had been elected president and that Roy Lee would be our vice-president. That was fine, but she went on to add, "I congratulate you class for making the right decision." I told you, she played favorites. Sorry, Roy Lee. Sara Gray was elected class secretary.

Near the end of our senior year, our academic rigor had slowed to a crawl, and we were just biding our time until graduation. One morning, Wist and I sought – and received – Miss Selma's permission to cut class so we could go to David's grandmother's house (she lived two blocks from the school) and play Monopoly. She told us what time we had to be back at school and then hurried off to Mr. Roark's office to "handle" our absence. Mr. Roark, our principal, bought Miss Selma's cover story, and our absence was excused. When David, Terry Weeks, yours truly, and our fourth, who was either Frank Timmins, John Bogue, or Mickey McCay, returned to the campus at the appointed time, Miss Selma met us at the edge of the campus and led us back into the school building through an isolated back door. She didn't want Mr. Roark to catch us. I think Terry won the Monopoly game that day, but Miss Selma won the hearts of four high school boys.

Miss Selma's off period coincided with my study hall. Ever the teacher, Miss Selma started retrieving me from study hall for one-on-one sessions with her in her empty classroom. She would have me read poems aloud that she had selected and then have me to expound on how I interpreted them. Knowing how she valued creative thinking, I actually enjoyed these exercises. Because I didn't worry about what was right or wrong, I just let my thoughts take sound. If her interpretation varied from mine, she would share it with me, and we would discuss both. I loved it.

The hardest session I experienced with this new learning format was when she had me read "To A Louse," by Scotland's Robert Burns. Burns wrote his works in the 1700s in a regional Scottish brogue, with bits of confusing Gaelic thrown in for good measure. Hard, hard reading. I remember Miss Selma laughing at me several times as I tried to read Burnsian prose. His words just didn't sound right when pronounced with a rural East Texas accent. We shared these sessions together for the entire semester, and I really hated to see them end.

Miss Selma gave me this extra time because she truly wanted to more fully develop my creative freedom. She was an inspired teacher, not a clock watcher who only viewed teaching as a job. She loved teaching, and I loved learning from her.

I have attended three of my high school reunions, my tenth, my 50th, and my 52nd high school reunions, and each was well-attended. It was inevitable, regardless of which reunion it was, that the discussion among the alumni would quickly get around to Miss Selma. A few other teachers' names would occasionally pop up, but memories of our beloved (and feared) Miss Selma basically held the floor. After more than 50 years, Miss Selma was still the undisputed star of the show. If that fact doesn't tell you what an impact teacher she was, let me confess one other testimony to the Selma mystique. I married Kay Hightower, who also was from Marshall, Texas, and who also took English under Selma Brotze. Even after more than fifty years of marriage, if Kay or I commit a grammatical error – either spoken or written – we look to the sky and apologize to Miss Selma. See, she's still with us. The impact powerful teachers can have on students is both mindboggling and eternal, teachers who extended themselves far beyond the norms to enrich lives, teachers like those I wrote about and others, including Lucile Estell, Agnes Menefee, Alline Miller, and Gussie Roughton, had very positive effects on many, many young people.

Chapter 13

An East Texas Ménage à Trois

I used to wonder where boys in New York City took their girlfriends to do their hugging, kissing, touching, and wishing. I had heard most NYC families didn't have – or particularly need – cars, so nighttime rides to some rural lover's lane seemed out of the question. I thought they might go to big parks like Central Park, but rumor had it they weren't all that safe. Some of the movies we saw showed kids cuddling and kissing on the roof-tops of their tenements or apartment buildings with a soothing chorus of cooing pigeons in the background. While I didn't know any boys from really big cities, I gave them credit for being creative enough to find places where they could snuggle in private. If their creativity failed them, I figured the fire that was charging through their veins as a result of puberty would magically steer them to secret places.

That same fire was rampaging through the veins of us East Texas boys, and our bodies and brains were being commanded by the alien known as puberty, just like our big-city counterparts. I was glad we didn't have those city-style obstacles to overcome in finding a quiet, private place to be alone with our "true" love. Wherever one was in Marshall, he was never more than three or four minutes from a dirt road that led to the isolation required for getting close to the love of his young life. Most of the dirt roads were courtesy of oil and gas companies who built them as service roads to producing oil or gas wells. East Texas was blessed with lots of oil and gas production, and that led to a plethora of lover's lane options. We called these nocturnal excursions into the fields and forests "parking."

Before the invention of automobiles, I think folks referred to this activity as "spooning" or maybe "sparking."

Kay Hightower (Senior Year). The Girl I Married More than 50 Years Ago

Never could figure out the "spooning" thing, but "sparking" made lots of sense to me. Some of those "sparks" probably ignited some raging fires. Now, before I share some actual parking episodes, I need to set the record straight. If a boy and a girl went parking, it in no way meant anything serious happened.

As a matter of fact, quite often, nothing – and I mean nothing – happened! Sometimes you sat with your date on the hood of the car and gazed into the sky, pondering what was beyond the stars. In most cases, you were trying to work up the nerve to kiss her, but even those "shy" nights were, at least, hand-holding nights. Also, they were often marked by thoughtful discussions and a gentility that led to a head-on-shoulder evening. Romantic, but not physical…yet. Those were nice evenings.

Most of us in East Texas were inoculated against sin with heavy doses of Protestant fundamentalism before we were turned loose into the world. However, the majority of us boys suppressed our church-inspired guilt and brimmed over with "want to." We were largely counterbalanced by girls brimming over with "can't do." The compromise lead to many nights of hugging, kissing, and sweating together. Nothing more. Those were nights where "can't do" trumped "want to." Incidentally, sweating and hugging went together in East Texas. The sweating wasn't necessarily the result of being hot-and-bothered. It was, more often than not, the result of hot East Texas nights with temperatures in the nineties, compounded by 90-plus humidity. Also, in the spirit of setting the record straight about parking, I need to say some pretty serious stuff sometimes went on in those pine thickets and on the dirt roads. You're not going to hear about any of those nitty-gritty, dirty boogie stories in this book. What happened in Marshall stays in Marshall.

I will tell you that one Saturday night, I was all spiffed up, reeking of English Leather (a popular cologne of the 1960s), and ready to head out on a date with my steady, when a dear friend stopped by to get last-minute tips on what to do on his date that evening. It was his first car date, and he was just short of breaking out in hives. My dad had him sit down and take some deep breaths. Daddy then had him splash on some of his Aqua Velva. Next, he asked my friend what his plans were and how much money he had. My pal told him they were going to the Paramount Theater and then probably to Neely's Drive-in for a Coke. I should tell you that it was the practice of the day in Marshall to call all soft drinks "Coke." After seeing how much money my bud had, Daddy asked me how much I had. I showed him my two dollars, and Daddy took one of the dollars and gave it to my friend. He told him to get some French fries to go with those Cokes. After my friend took off on his date, I complained that I didn't have but a dollar left for my date. Daddy said for me to skip the movie this particular night and go straight to the parking part of our date. I was taken aback because I had no idea Daddy knew we were into parking. I picked up my date, and we did as Daddy had told us to do. We then went to Neely's and spent my remaining dollar.

The next day, I asked my brother, Robert, who was home from college, how Daddy knew I'd been going parking. Robert told me it was because Daddy always found goat weeds in the grill of our car the morning after each of my dates. For those of you that have never encountered goat weed, suffice it to say that if you drive into an East Texas field, you WILL get goat weed in your grill. Daddy was a smart old bird.

In most cases, parking left one with any number of different feelings, ranging from exhilaration to frustration, from elation to depression. Boys and girls didn't always go home from a parking session with the same conclusions. Plus, a really good night of necking could be overshadowed by surprise events that completely changed the mood of the post-parking ride home; case in point: a dead battery.

One night, my date and I took a dirt road off of Sue Belle Lake Road, a tar-topped winding road on the Northern outskirts of Marshall. We meandered some distance back into the woods before we chose our little love nest. I killed the motor, and we snuggled up to each other and went about our kissing as Floyd Kramer's piano softly emanated from the car radio. This scenario played out for some time, and we were probably on our 15th song when, just as Fats Domino was about to tell us where he found his thrill, the radio went silent. Reluctant to break the mood, I tried to ignore what I knew caused the dead radio. The battery was dead, which meant the car was dead. The third thing to die with the battery and the car was.... well, use your imagination. We were stranded in the middle of a field. We had a problem.

I told my girlfriend I would have to walk about a mile or so to the nearest house and call Daddy to come give our battery a jump start. She chose to walk with me rather than lock herself in the car and wait for my return. The call was made from a nearby farmhouse and, after using my predicament to get laughs from all our visiting family members, Daddy agreed to come to our rescue. He told us to wait at the intersection of the dirt road and Sue Belle Lake Road. We stood there swatting mosquitos for what seemed like hours before Daddy finally showed up. His showing up was the good news. The bad news was that my brother, Homer, and my Uncle Lawrence, who lived in Houston accompanied him. My date and I shared the back seat with Homer, and I directed Daddy through the forest to our private spot in a remote field. During the entire ride back to the dead car, I detected the sly smiles on the faces of Daddy, Homer, and Uncle Lawrence. No eye contact, just little know-it-all grins. I was embarrassed, and my date was mortified. I reached over and took her hand to reassure her everything would be fine. She didn't respond. In fact, her hand felt like a dead fish, and she never even glanced in my direction. I knew resuscitating this romance would be a major challenge.

Experiences like the dead battery taught me a couple of things. First, when you're parking in the middle of nowhere, never leave your radio on once you've killed the ignition. Second, if you're on a date and have car trouble and you have to call Daddy for help, insist he come alone. I scored two "learning experiences" that troublesome night.

Before I leave this parking tale, let me tell you about a similar one that involved Brother Homer and his high school girlfriend. He, like me, had followed one of those dirt roads into the middle of a field with lovin' on his mind. Once he was deep in the woods, he drifted off the dirt road and let the left side of the car miss the cattle guard that forded a rather deep gully running through the field. A cattle guard is a bridge laid across a sizable ditch or gully designed to allow vehicles to cross it while preventing cattle from doing so. It is made by welding a series of pipes on girders that run from one edge of the gully to the other. The pipes have gaps between them and are round, making it impossible for a cow to cross it. I'm sure Homer's excitement about finding the perfect spot for necking distracted his attention from the perils of the dirt road. Regardless of why he ran off the cattle guard, he did. The 1949 Ford was half off the rails and half on, causing it to teeter with each movement of Homer or his date. They scooted out of the passenger side of the Ford, walked to a phone, and called Daddy for help. When Daddy finally found Homer and the balancing car, he couldn't come up with a quick and easy solution. Therefore, he and Homer took his date home and decided to salvage the Ford from the cattle guard the next day. Daddy's displeasure was intensely amplified when he found out the girl lived in Carthage, a small town thirty miles south of Marshall. The next day, Daddy hired a wrecker, and he and the driver somehow saved the Ford from falling into the gully. Repairs to the underside of the Ford were required, but the car was saved. Daddy and Homer had several private meetings about this episode during which Daddy "calmly" explained the advantages of paying attention when driving and the wisdom of dating girls who lived in your hometown. Subtlety wasn't Daddy's strong suit, so his "explanations" left no doubts as to his expectations.

The last story I'm going to share with you in this chapter involved me and Kay Hightower, the girl I've now been married to for more than fifty-three years, and, yes, I have her permission to tell this story.

One beautiful East Texas night, Kay and I found ourselves parked in the middle of a pasture not far off Rosborough Springs Road, just south of Marshall. As usual, it was hot and humid and, since my 1955 Ford didn't have air conditioning, all our windows were down in hopes an unexpected breeze might find us. It didn't; but we found each other, and some pretty serious hugging and kissing ensued. Right about the time our arms and minds became fully involved in our passion, an uninvited surprise visitor joined us in the front seat.

Perhaps because we were preoccupied, we failed to hear the approach of a fully-grown, black and white Holstein cow. This curious cow not only approached our car, it, unbeknownst to us, quietly stuck its entire head in the driver's side window. It then announced itself with a loud snort and a generous spraying of slimy slobber that went all over both of us. The bovine blitzkrieg and accompanying snort took us both by total – and I do mean total – surprise. Fear and shock caused us to straighten, scream, and offer rapid-fire prayers for our safety. Our screams and attempts to straighten up caused the now-frightened and confused cow to also panic. It started bellowing and violently jerking its head, trying desperately to get it out of this tight space it found itself sharing with two out-of-control, screaming humans. Sheer chaos and an old Ford full of shrieking, flailing, and bellowing held sway until the cow finally got its head back out of the window. Old Bossy didn't just gallop away from the car, she broke into an all-out, udder-swinging sprint in search of safer ground, bawling frantically until she disappeared into a pine thicket as far away from us as she could get.

When Kay and I finally caught our breath and calmed down, we left our ill-chosen lover's lane and headed for Mr. Cargill's Gulf service station on Pinecrest Drive, where we washed off the cow slobber as best we could. I don't know if the Holstein suffered cardiac arrest or later realized the humor of the situation it got itself into. The humor stuck with Kay and me, as we have shared laughter about our memorable East Texas ménage à trois many times over the last fifty or so years.

Chapter 14

Neely's on Grand

When Ricky Nelson sang "Waitin' in School" in 1957, he told us how, when school was out, all the kids went to the drug store at the corner of Lincoln and 46th to hang out, "throw a nickel in the jukebox," and dance. On "Happy Days," Richie, Ralph Malph, Potsie, and the Fonz all gathered at Arnold's, which later became Al's. In his 1957 classic, "School Days," Chuck Berry tells us:

> "Soon as three o'clock rolls around
> You finally lay your burden down
> Close up your books, get out of your seat
> Down the hall and into the street
> Up to the corner and 'round the bend
> Right to the juke joint you go in…"

You get the picture. Teens seem to always anoint an unofficial hang-out where they can gather with their peers to gossip, flirt, giggle, show-off, grab a soda, maybe dance, and just be seen. In Marshall, it was Neely's Drive-In on Grand Avenue (U.S. Highway 80).

A little history is in order. Neely Brothers' Brown Pig was opened in 1927 by Lonnie and Mamie Neely, who sold their sandwiches at a gas station on the west end of Marshall. As the name implies, its specialty was barbecued pork sandwiches dubbed, "Brown Pigs." The place quickly established itself as home to the finest barbecued pork sandwiches in East Texas and became "the" hang-out for Marshall kids. In 1933, Neely's moved to a building on Grand Avenue that was owned by the family of football great, Y. A. Tittle.

During the 1940s and 1950s, my older brothers, Homer and Robert, were fixtures at Neely's during their high school and college years. As a matter of fact, Homer was attending East Texas Baptist College (now university) in 1954 when he proposed to his girlfriend, "Freddie," at Neely's. Freddie, who was really Fredonia Jordan from Lufkin, Texas, was a vivacious, pretty cheerleader who was also attending East Texas Baptist. When Homer brought Freddie into Neely's on proposal night, he had co-opted Mr. and Mrs. Neely into the plan to surprise his bride-to-be. When she ordered her normal Coke, Mr. Neely brought it to her in a tall glass. As usual, the glass contained the Coke and ice cubes. Only this time, one of the ice cubes had the engagement ring frozen inside it. The Neelys had taken the ring from Homer that afternoon and frozen it into the "special" ice cube. After some coaching, Freddie discovered the ring and started laughing, squealing, and crying at the same time. Mr. Neely then announced the engagement to all his customers, and Homer and Freddie were the stars of that evening. By the way, the Cokes were on the house that night. The engagement "took," as they say, and the marriage lasted forty-eight years until Homer died at age seventy. Mr. and Mrs. Neely were nice people and treated their young customers as though they were family.

By the time I started driving and hanging out at Neely's in the early 1960s, the restaurant had moved about a mile east on Grand Avenue (U.S. Highway 80). They had moved into a nice building that had once housed the short-lived K & M Restaurant, owned by a fellow named Marvin Kendrick. Marvin also owned a bait shop a couple of doors down from his eatery. I'm not so sure that was a good idea. The thought of him getting his worms and his spaghetti mixed-up might have hung in the backs of potential clients' minds.

The new Neelys had seven booths and six tables for inside dining and a large downward-sloping parking area that accommodated all customers and offered curb service. Except for the asphalt apron encircling the new building, the massive parking lot was dirt, or, more accurately, East Texas red clay. It had no lined spaces or parking rules, so teens filled up the lot by squeezing in any way possible. Cars pointed all directions. If you were hemmed in and wanted to leave, well, tough luck. Untangling the chaotic mass of steel just to let one car out wasn't on the menu. While the Neely's parking lot had its off-the-wall charms, it had some problems, too. For example, Marshall got (and still does get) forty-seven inches of rain a year, and, when it came, it usually came in the form of heavy thunderstorms. No Seattle-style drizzles in Marshall; we had gully washers. Well, these torrential downpours transformed this unpaved parking lot into something akin to the bumper car ride at the county fair. Cars frequently became stuck and slid around in search of traction on the slick, clay-covered inclines. The rains also drained down through the parking lot, creating major wide and deep ruts that were difficult for smaller cars to ride through or over. The ruts were never repaired, so each rain widened and deepened the mini-ravines. If the Mormons' covered wagons had been required to cross Neely's parking lot during their trek to the West, they would have never made it to Utah. Despite these issues, Neely's had a lock on first place in the hearts of Marshall and its teens.

Townspeople who needed their Brown Pig fix usually ate inside or took their delicacies home, leaving the parking lot to the young folks. Several kids worked as carhops at Neely's through the years. The one I best remember was David Ponder, a smallish boy my age who was rather quiet and somber as he went about delivering cokes and fries to the rowdy teens. I also remember he rode his bike to and from work, and he lived several miles out on U.S. 59. He was a hard-working boy, and, even when customers gave David a hard time, he kept his cool and took care of business. His handling of his business in the face of obstacles put in his way by smart-aleck kids earned him tons of respect among his peers. I can't remember for sure, but I suspect David made very, very little from the tips he received from his cash-strapped classmate-customers. I recently located David, retired and living in Waskom, Texas, a tiny town about 16 miles east of Marshall. After apologizing to him for my failure to tip him better in high school, I promised I would take him to lunch my next trip to East Texas. I won't forget. It will be good to see him.

If David or some other teen wasn't car hopping, his spot was taken by Mr. Neely, the owner. The kids were a lot nicer to Mr. Neely than they were to the other carhops. He had a low tolerance for wise-cracking, smart-ass boys, and no one wanted to be taken off Mr. Neely's welcome list. The social humiliation would have been devastating.

The sandwiches at Neely's were divine. Tucker Conley, a quick-witted classmate of mine, once told me he thought the Neelys laced their sandwiches with cocaine or some powerfully addictive drug. For sure, something kept everyone coming back for a shot of barbecue heaven. I had three cousins who lived in and around Waco, Texas, who, at least quarterly, drove the 236 miles from Waco to Marshall just to fill up on Brown Pigs. My cousin Ann O'Bannon and her daughters, Pat and Sue, lived in Marshall prior to the late 1950s and had become hardened devotees of Brown Pigs, which they called "Neely Burgers." On these barbecue runs, they would first visit Neely's to "pig out," then visit the cemetery to pay their respects to their dead relatives, then come by our house for a quick visit and, lastly, return to Neely's to eat again and load up on "Neely Burgers" to take back to Waco. The priority for their visits to Marshall was never in doubt. They were here for their fix.

One night, Butch Kennedy and I cruised Grand Avenue, and, instead of talking about sports or girls, we were lusting for Brown Pigs. We lamented that we never had our fill of the barbecue treasures, usually running out of money before we were full. Well, this particular night, Butch announced that he was "loaded," and we were going to Neely's to eat as many Brown Pigs as we could hold. We did just that. I topped out at six sandwiches, and Butch managed eight before crying "uncle." Brown pigs made pigs out of everyone who ate them. Addictive? Absolutely!

The Neely family had a substantial presence in Marshall when I was growing up, but the face of Neely's Drive-In on Grand was James Neely. James had eight siblings, most of whom branched out and tried their hands at the barbecue business, but it was James who ran the original family business and kept the fame and reputation of Neely's and Brown Pigs alive and prospering. James and his wife, Frances, worked tirelessly at the restaurant, and their twin daughters, Francene and Geraldine, who were one year younger than me, were fixtures at the restaurant through their teens. They could often be seen doing their homework in the booth closest to the kitchen. It was a family affair and had been since 1927. All of us local kids felt a closeness to Neely's and with the Neely Family. It was like they had accepted us into their family. Perhaps the best way to illustrate this "closeness" is to tell you that when our 50th class reunion rolled around, we held registration and our convening dinner under a large tent erected in the parking lot (still dirt) at Neely's on Grand. What was on the menu? Brown Pigs, of course. I ate three of them.

Another of the Neely brothers, Arvil, hung around East Texas, trying his hand at the restaurant and barbecue business in several different towns, including Kilgore and Liberty. The first of his ventures I remember was when he opened an A&W Root Beer Drive-In on Marshall's South Washington Street. The idea was great, the product was terrific, and the location was pretty good. It should have worked. The problem was the owner, Arvil. While his brother, James, built a huge clientele with efficiency, kindness, and a family feeling at his drive-in, Arvil just couldn't relax and let success come his way. He didn't care for kids, was tight as a tick, distrustful of anyone under thirty, and was grouchy. Other than that, he was a very nice man.

A customer could either walk in and order at a window or stay in the car for curb service. My friend, David Wist, once entered the building to order at the window. He was smoking at the time, and Arvil told him he didn't allow smoking. Offended by Arvil's no smoking policy, David ground out his cigarette on the floor. An argument ensued, and Arvil ended-up calling the police on David. David could be an argumentative wise-ass, and Arvil always took the bait. David was banned from ever coming back to A&W Root Beer on South Washington.

The star of Arvil's menu was the root beer, which was served in frosted mugs. The mugs came in two sizes, regular and small. The children's mugs were particularly cute, and, early on, some of them must have been swiped by customers because Arvil watched them like a hawk. The minute a customer finished his or her root beer, Arvil magically appeared to reclaim his mug. I often wondered if Arvil's fear of being ripped-off was the result of his eight brothers and sisters having taken his toys from him when he was a little boy. He seemed to live in fear of his customers going home with mugs, salt and pepper shakers, or plastic french fry baskets. A friend, Jerry Cargill, worked for Arvil one summer and told all of his friends to be sure to break our plastic spoons and forks in half after using them, as Arvil would wash and re-use any returned intact.

Late in his life, Arvil opened a restaurant in Marshall called Porky's. It served sandwiches called Porky Pigs that were great. They were obviously made from the original Neely barbecue sauce recipe. At Porky's, Arvil didn't have to put up with unruly teens. In this new setting, he mellowed out and became the perfect gentleman. He served his food on paper plates and his drinks in paper cups, so thievery wasn't a worry. He and David Wist even patched things up. Only recently, I learned that Arvil had spent time in an enemy prisoner-of-war camp during World War II. Who knows what horrid memories be brought home with him?

Any ex-Marshallite who returns to Marshall for a visit is a cinch to stop by Neely's on Grand for a nostalgic visit, a Brown Pig or two, and a bag of the mouth-watering sandwiches to go. Neely's is now owned by Ray Fessler, a high school classmate of mine. He has decorated the dining room with pictures from the golden days of Neely's. The last time I was there, I saw a picture of my wife, Kay, in her high school pep squad outfit. Wow! No wonder I fell for her.

Ray's barbecue isn't made from the old Neely recipe, but it's still powerfully good stuff. Can't wait for my next Brown Pig.

Chapter 15

From Corvettes to the White Flash

I cannot imagine writing a book about my teen years in the late 1950s and early 1960s without including a chapter on the cars of that era. Somewhere else in this book, I mentioned that I believed that, as a community, Marshall was in its heyday in the '50s and '60s. Well, now I further assert that I think that same time period was the heyday of the American automobile.

Today, the new car models are difficult to tell apart from the 1999 models. It's as though all of the innovative automotive design engineers went on an extended sabbatical at the same time and have failed to return to their drafting boards. Lincolns look like Mitsubishis, and BMWs look like Hyundais. The descriptive word that comes to mind is "boring." That bland uniformity was not in evidence when I was in high school. The foreign car invasion had landed on our shores back then but with moderation. Mercedes Benz, MG, Volkswagen, Fiat, Opel, Triumph, and a few other foreign makes could be spotted on our streets, but they were looked upon as novelties. The streets of Marshall belonged to Detroit, with General Motors, Ford, and Chrysler the undisputed kings of the road. American Motors tried to keep up with the big three but with little success. Cars manufactured by Studebaker, Packard, Hudson, Crosley, Nash, Kaiser, and Willys made cameo appearances during those heady days. Boys talked about Holley carburetors, Hurst gear shifters on the floor, cubic inches, Hollywood mufflers, turning knobs that attached to the steering wheel, four-speed transmissions, chrome tailpipe extenders, glass packs, trip deuces, and many other "cool" accessories to make cars go faster and look better while doing so.

One thing that made the cars of the '50s and '60s such a big part of our culture was that each car company produced cars that were unique in appearance to their brand. Only the nerdiest of boys couldn't identify the manufacturer, model, and year of any car he spotted. Most boys could identify the carmaker by just listening to it start. Each make of car had its own start-up signature, with Chrysler products having the most distinctive "voice." American Motor's makes were not so identifiable by sound because they often didn't start. Another reason cars were enormously popular in those days was because they generated tremendous interest and discussion with the introduction of each year's model. New models and innovations in style and engineering were page one stories and the topics of endless discussions among the citizenry. In advertising, the objective has long been to create top-of-mind awareness about your product among your consumer base. Detroit in the 1950s -1960s was on top of its marketing game.

The last reason I'll offer as to why cars were in their heyday when I was in high school was the race among carmakers to "out horsepower" the competition. Having the fastest car was a badge of honor, highly sought after by manufacturers and car freaks alike. I was never a true, died-in-the-wool car guy, so I can't offer facts and figures about which car had how much horsepower or how many cubic inches. I can, however, name a handful of boys from wealthy families in Marshall who bought the fastest models to come out each year.

Ronnie Snider, Jackie Carson, Carlisle Langley, and Bobby Whelan were the frontrunners in the competition to have the fastest cars each year. I remember Ronnie having a very fast 1955 black and white Corvette, along with a '59 white Chevy Impala Super Sport you needed a pilot's license to operate. Ronnie was a two-car speeder, as he souped-up an old Ford that he used for racing at the various dragstrips. Of course, Ronnie drove it at nearly full speed whether he was on the dragstrip, Highway 43, or Bomar Street. A local highway patrol officer, James Wedding, was in a constant state of vexation because he never could catch Ronnie. The chase-to-no-avail scenario played out enough times for it to become known as the Snider – Wedding Race. In truth, it reminded me of Jackie Gleason's futile effort to catch Burt Reynolds in *Smokey and the Bandit*. If that comparison doesn't work for you, how about Roscoe P. Coltrain's unsuccessful stabs at catching the Duke boys in the television series, *The Dukes of Hazard?*

Jerry Cargill told me a Ronnie story that bears repeating. It seems Ronnie was in his old Ford, driving wide-open on Highway 43 between Tatum and Marshall when Patrolman Wedding passed him going the opposite direction. The officer did a fast turnaround and set out to nab

Ronnie. Ronnie knew Wedding was in hot pursuit, so when he got to the intersection of Pinecrest Drive – which was Highway 43 when it got into Marshall – and Bomar Street, Ronnie spun into a Texaco station that was on the corner. He quickly ran his Ford into an unoccupied bay, jumped out, and sent his car to the ceiling by raising the grease rack. He then lowered the bay door and sat on the floor. Wedding never found him that night, and his Snider-induced anxiety became more acute.

Carlisle Langley ran through a series of fast new cars, including a Mustang, a '61 Pontiac Bonneville, and a '63 Plymouth with a 426 horsepower Hemi engine and all the 4-barrel carburetors that could be crammed under the hood. That Plymouth was incredibly fast, and it was frightening to think of that much power in Carlisle's Langley's hand. Carlisle often defied convention when he was young. Whatever he was, he was fearless, and speed was one of the tonics that spurred him on.

Bobby Whelan also had a '63 Plymouth with a 426 Hemi. It was a beautiful bright red, and Bobby claimed it was a chick magnet. Bobby loved to drag race his car, and, one night, I rode in his car when he raced another speed-machine out on Elysian Fields Highway. I rode with him once. Never again. The Plymouth was light on its feet, and it had hyper-sensitive steering. Bobby had to constantly fight to keep it on the road. He won the race, but he lost me as a co-pilot.

Bobby's younger brother, John, who was my age and didn't necessarily have the fastest cars, but he drove everything he owned at full speed most all of the time. John had high octane fuel running through his veins. Whether he was driving a Jeep or his Plymouth Sport Fury, it felt like it could fly because of his driving. John ended up raising cattle and counting oil money, but he should have been a race car driver. Everyone thought he should be racing at Daytona Speedway, not Five Notch Road in Marshall. He was an incredibly gifted driver. Every time I rode with him, I got out of his car, both glad to be back on *terra firma* and amazed at his driving skills. Finally, I got to where I just wouldn't ride with John. I figured that as good of a driver as he was, he had taken enough high-speed risks to be tempting fate. I would just sit it out as he sped his way toward legendary status among Marshall's speedsters.

You know, it just dawned on me that all four of the speedsters I just wrote about were adrenalin junkies as teens and young men. They lived their lives like they were propelled by trip-deuce carburetors and four-on-the-floor. Ronnie Snider went on to become a huge success in the lumber business, but I wonder if he ever got over his need for speed before he succumbed to lung cancer. Bobby Whelan was murdered by his wife, Lola Faye, who then took her own life. John Whelan died young of a massive heart attack. Carlisle Langley found Christ and became a wonderful family man before dying in 2018.

Some Marshallites claim the fastest car in Marshall during the early '60s was Wayne's Bogue's red 1961 Ford Galaxy Starliner. It was fast from the factory, but the guy who owned it before Wayne, Sonny Griffin, had sent it to a speed shop in Houston for "tweaking." The speed shop was famous for maximizing the performance of NASCAR racers. No one was certain what the speed shop did to the Ford, but everyone agreed that it came back to Marshall itching to run. Wayne and his two chief running buddies, Leslie Lawrence and Rodney Burkham were steady cruisers of Grand Avenue (U.S. Highway 80), always on the lookout for a race for Wayne's Ford. Wayne, Leslie, Rodney, and Ed McHam were probably the premier gearheads in our class of 1964.

According to Leslie, Wayne's car was dethroned as the fastest car in town when Buddy Ford bought his maroon 1963 Chevrolet 409 four-speed with two 4-barrel carburetors. Buddy, accompanied by his friend, Jerry Foley, bought the hot car from Rudd Chevrolet in Waskom, Texas, one day and raced it in the Hallsville Drag Races the next. So much for breaking in a car before pushing it to its limits. Jerry tells me they won the race in Hallsville. Shocker.

While researching for this chapter, I talked to my old friends Leslie Lawrence and Jerry Foley, both of whom were, are, and shall forever be addicted to old cars and fast cars. When I talked to Jerry, he was watching a car auction on television, and I reached Leslie at his auto shop near Gilmer, Texas. He rebuilds old cars and makes most of them go faster. Even though they are both now in their seventies, I'll bet they still have grease under their fingernails and their hearts go into overdrive at hearing the throaty sound of a well-tuned engine with twin four-barrel carbs.

There were other guys in Marshall with cars that had been hyped-up to run faster than the factory had intended. Carol Mayfield had a black '57 Chevrolet Bel Air two-door that was both very fast and good looking. Turkey Boaze had a high-powered '63 Chevy like Buddy's Ford's, so he didn't lose many races. Dick Cole, the best mechanic in Marshall (at least I thought so), jazzed up a 1958 Chevy Biscayne that was deceptively fast. Dick paid dearly to be my good friend. He's who I called late at night more than once when my car broke down. Thank you, Dick. Ed McHam also burned rubber around Marshall with his juiced '58 Impala Super

Sport. Jackie Carson had a black Corvette that was more than he could handle. He often had Dick Cole or Ladd Moore drive him around in it because he really didn't know how to drive it, and it intimidated him.

Eventually, he became comfortable with it, but I still never rode with him. I was uncomfortable with him being comfortable with that much energy under his control. To me, the 1958 Chevrolet Impala Super Sport convertible was the all-time winner of cars that combined looks with performance. I remember just sitting and staring at Boonie Solomon's bright red one on more than one occasion. Perfection on wheels.

Not all great cars of my high school years were built for speed. Scotty Gray had an over-the-moon baby blue Metropolitan, a two-seater that always brought a smile to your face. I was too tall to fit in it, but Scotty was built like his car and looked like he belonged in it. I thought it was more like a pet than a car. They were a perfect match. Jerry Cargill had a '51 Ford Victoria coupe that was blue and white. Every time I saw him drive by in his cool car with Narcissa Moore snuggled up next to him, I thought, man, Cargill's got it going on in his life. Speaking of old Fords, Charlie Starke had a nice '49 Ford he kept spotless. He took the Ford to college with him. However, one Friday night, he and Leneda Kay were driving from Stephen F. Austin University to Marshall for the weekend, when, while passing through the Sabine River bottom, they ran head-on into a large bull that had escaped its owner's fence. Leneda nearly died from the crash, Charlie suffered some injuries, and his little Ford was totaled. David Applebaum had a 1951 Chevrolet coupe that was as basic as a car could be, but it looked great because he had it painted a metallic blue that made it shine like a gemstone. I probably could have outrun it on foot, but it really did look fine. Another car I lusted after was Robert Sullivan's canary yellow '58 Ford convertible. If there was ever a car designed for wowing the ladies, it was that one.

Tucker Conley's dad owned a high-end used car lot, so he got to drive lots of cool cars. One day he'd be cruising grand in an MG convertible, and the next, you might see him in a '57 Chevy Bel Air coupe. One time I went to Mr. Conley's lot and fell in love with a '56 Ford Crown Victoria. Believe it or not, it was pink and white with black and white rolled leather seats. I was in love, momentarily forgetting the fact that Daddy would never let me drive a pink car. I asked Mr. Conley the price of the car. He looked at me for an uncomfortable amount of time. He then looked at the car for an equal amount of time. I guess he was mentally assessing my financial ability to buy and, perhaps, what Daddy might say or do to him if he sold me a pink car. His response to my price inquiry was, "Scotty, it's too much ninety-five." He was right. It was a bad fit.

Since both of my parents worked, it was necessary for me to have my own car. I always had after-school sports practices or a job, so I needed a car to get to and from school or work. I got my first car in the ninth-grade, a 1950 Chevrolet sedan that was the ugliest shade of brown known to man. It had at one time been an Army staff car, accounting for the drab brown color. It had large metal sun visors attached to the roof, which may have endeared it to the Army but did little to impress me. I knew I was lucky to have a car, so I never dared complain to Mother or Daddy.

One day, the brakes went completely out as I was driving to school. I managed to gear it down, kill the motor, and coast into a parking spot about four blocks from the high school. After school, I drove it the half mile or so to our athletic facilities where I had track practice. The same stopping procedure allowed me to park it on the edge of the football practice field. When practice was over, Paul Wood, Roy Lee Fry, and a forgotten fourth member of our track team decided to try to make it to the Dairy Queen on Grand Avenue. Knowing I had no brakes, we decided to leave our spiked track shoes on for the ride. Our plan for having to stop the car was to slow it as much as possible by down-shifting and then for each of us to open a door and use our spikes to bring the car to a halt. I know. I know. That was a maximum stupid plan. We dodged all the stops until we got to the stoplight at Grand and Alamo, right in front of the Dairy Queen. Before we could take our left at the light to get to the DQ, the light turned red, necessitating a stop. I had brought the Chevy to a near stop, but we were still rolling. In unison, we opened our doors and planted our spikes into the asphalt. Also in unison, we screamed at the pain we had inflicted upon ourselves. Our plan failed miserably, and we slowly rolled into the middle of the intersection. We didn't care where the car ended up. We were concerned with whether we would ever walk again. Fortunately, we escaped without injury from what could have been a ligament demolition derby. I made it home late that afternoon, bringing my old Chevy to a stop by running it into a hedgerow that was at the end of the dead-end street on which I lived. When I told Daddy the story of how we tried to cope with no brakes, he expressed serious concern as to whether I would ever be able to think my way through life.

On a lark, Daddy bought a low mileage, one-owner, four-door, baby blue 1950 Cadillac. I drove it on some dates, falsely thinking the extra seat room it afforded might come in handy. It was definitely luxurious inside, but it was, without a doubt, born from the union of a Sherman tank and a Mack truck. It was heavy, really heavy. One night, my date and I went to the Capri Drive-In movie in the Caddy. When the movie was over, I cranked up and pulled into the exit lane. Unbeknownst to me, I had forgotten to return my speaker to its stand. It was still hooked on my driver's side window. The Caddy's glass was so strong it never broke and, instead, the Caddy pulled the entire speaker stand and the ball of concrete that served as its buried anchor out of the ground and drug it with us into the exit lane. When I stopped to sheepishly separate my car from the drive-in's speaker and its resting place, I got a lot of looks that visually called me "dumb ass." Dadburn it. The car was so massive, and my date was so small, she could barely see over the dashboard.

At the end of my sophomore year, my brother, Robert, who was teaching high school in New Orleans at the time, bought a new car and gave me his '55 Ford. It was white with a bright red interior. It was also very, very peppy and had a stick shift. I didn't race it, but I loved having the power, which allowed me to show-off once in a while. Within my circle of friends, my Ford became known as the White Flash. When my muffler got a hole in it, Daddy took it to Sears automotive and, to my surprise, had the shot muffler replaced with a glass pack muffler. For the uninitiated, a glass pack has a beautiful rumble sound when it burns out a bit. It sounded super cool. Thanks, Dad.

Daddy was always unimpressed with the importance I placed on the impact a great car could have on my image among my peers. For example, when I lost the moon disk hub cap from my right rear wheel, I expected Daddy to get me a new one. Instead, he opened my trunk, took out my tire tool, and popped off the right front hub cap. He then tossed the tire tool and the hub cap into the trunk, closed its lid, and headed for the house. When I complained about the White Flash looking crippled, he said that now each side had its own look; one side with hub caps and the other without. He added that if I wanted to ride by Neely's and look cool, I just needed to make certain I rode by going west to east so the side with two hubcaps would always show. Huh? Daddy's solution was unsatisfactory to me, but it wasn't up for debate. It was non-negotiable to him. Eventually, I found a used, matching hubcap at Cap Solomon's junkyard and parts store. It cost me six dollars, but it was worth it to return the White Flash to its full glory.

The first summer after inheriting the White Flash, I got a highway construction job with Jordan Construction out of Lufkin, Texas. The highway we were building ran between DeBerry, Texas, and Carthage, Texas. My route to the worksite took me through the tiny hamlet of Elysian Fields, and it generally took me about thirty minutes each way. I had to be at work by 7 a.m., and I would return home about 6 p.m. My very first morning of driving to work, I drove by a cluster of three houses on the Elysian Fields highway, and a small group of black teenaged boys standing under a pine tree pelted my car with large pine cones. The same group of boys was in one of the yards as I drove home from work. As I sped by their houses, I honked and shot them the jolly roger. This exchange of unpleasantries went on every day for several weeks until one day, I ran slap out of gas just as I was about to pass their spot. The White Flash sputtered, coughed, and coasted to a stop right in front of the four cone-tossing teens. I was resigned to getting my butt whipped, but I couldn't just lock myself in the car and wait on the Lone Ranger to rescue me. As I slowly got out of the car, the boys just stared at me. With few options available, I walked over to them and asked if there was a phone I could use. To my surprise, one of the boys walked me into a house from which I called my mother and asked her to bring me some gas. She did. While waiting for her, I leaned against my car, and the boys settled under the pine tree. We never spoke a word. When Mother arrived, I gassed-up, and we went home. Guess what? The very next morning, they bombed me again with pine cones. Going home that evening, I honked at them and again gave them the finger. Things were back to normal.

One Friday afternoon, after our Maverick baseball team had just beat Longview 4–2, Danny Love said he would come by and pick me up to go cruising that night. His family had just bought a new 1962 Chevrolet, and he was eager to take it out for the first time. On schedule, Danny picked me up, and off we went in search of girls to take riding in the Love's new wheels. We made one quick cruise up and down Grand, two circles around the square, and headed south on South Washington Street.

Scotty and Shadow with White Flash in the background.

We were laughing about something, and Danny took his eyes off the road. The next thing we knew, we had jumped the curb, hit a section of broken, jagged concrete curbing, and blown both right-side tires. We had come to a very rough and bumpy landing, making us think we had damaged more than two tires. Danny was petrified about the punishment his mother and sister, Betty, would lay on him. He slowly walked across the street to Sullivan's Funeral Home and called home for instructions. A wrecker was called for the new car, and I took Danny home. It was a short night. His driving privileges were suspended for a while, but, eventually, he made it back to the streets.

Cars have been integral parts of high school boys' social lives as long as there have been boys and cars. Before the automobile came on the scene, a fellow needed a wagon or, at least, a horse to facilitate his courting. I'm a bit out of my depth trying to talk about pre-car dating, but I can tell you with some confidence that walking dates just didn't cut it in the '50s and '60s. I mentioned horses because Daddy, who was raised on a very rural farm, told me his first few dates were on his old horse, Dan. I guess you just pulled your date up behind you and rode off to wherever you went to do whatever you did on dates back then.

I can't speak for everyone of my generation, but I can tell you I, personally, am very glad that the majority of the cars of my era did not have bucket seats. When I look at most of the cars on the road today, the majority seem to have bucket seats and very little legroom in the back seat. I'm not too surprised young people are waiting longer to get married, and the birth rate has dropped. Figure it out. Studies show that most people consider their car to be their most private space on earth. I don't know about that for sure, but when you are dating while you are in high school, it darn sure is.

One thing I often did when I was in high school was busy myself with "ride-bys." By ride-bys, I mean I spent an inordinate amount of time and gasoline just driving by the houses of girls I had crushes on. In retrospect, I realize the ride-by gambit was a total waste of time and gas. I never stopped. Perhaps, I was just hoping the girl of my dreams would see me and run out of her house to flag me down so she could profess her love for me. Never happened. But, I'll bet you I'm not the only boy who pursued this form of courtship. Sometimes, I wonder if any of the girls ever noticed my ride-bys. At least it wouldn't have been a total waste of gas and time. Did you ever even notice my ride-bys, Joan Steele, Barbara Young, Pam Shepherd? Well, did you?

Chapter 16

The Bob Hope Motel, Bouree, and Cajun Baseball

No. This is not a chapter about the comedian Bob Hope and a motel he owned. It's a story about a motel in Marshall, Texas, built by a businessman named Robert "Bob" Hope and the role it played in the lives of a group of teenage boys in the late 1950s and early 1960s. The Bob Hope Motel was perfectly situated at the intersection of U.S. Highways 59 and 80 and State Highway 43. On land where U.S. Highway 80, U.S. Highway 59, and Texas State Highway 43. In modern real estate lingo, it had three things going for it: location, location, location. Robert and his wife, Christine, built the thirty-unit tourist court motel in 1948. While the history of the Hope family is interesting and an important part of Marshall's history, this chapter will only concern itself with their motel and the significant part it played as the home base for a few years for a bunch of boys struggling to become men.

Robert and Christine Hope intersected with my life because they were the grandparents of my dear friends David Wist and his older brother, Bobby. Their mother was Anne Hope Wist. Robert died in 1950, leaving his widow, Christine – whom we all called "Neenie" because Bobby and David called her "Neenie" – the big job of running the Bob Hope Motel by herself. Since David and Bobby spent lots and lots of time at the motel with Neenie, so did their friends. Neenie was a lady of ample girth and prone to passing on exercise such as walking, so she liked having the boys around to run errands such as taking ice or towels to the rooms. Neenie was also crazy about David and Bobby and generally gave them free run of the motel. Oh, she tried to control them by occasionally screaming and hollering at them but, in the end, she let them have their way. Bobby could always sweet talk Neenie into doing things his way. When any of us spent the night with either brother, we got to stay in a motel room. Doing so was pretty heady stuff for young teens. It made us feel free and empowered, both of which were exhilarating.

My visits to Bob Hope Motel were sporadic, though not infrequent, until the 1961-1962 school year. That was Bobby Wist's senior year and my sophomore year in high school. While my friendship with Davis was always strong, Bobby and I became very close that year and spent lots of time together. The Wist boys' dad had been sent to New Roads, Louisiana, by his employer, Brown & Root, to oversee a major construction project that was to take about two years to complete. Mrs. Wist joined her husband in New Roads, and they leased out their house in Marshall for two years. Bobby and David, not wanting to change schools, moved in with Neenie at the motel. She gave them room number twenty-one to live in until they could re-join their parents for the summer. Living in #21 gave the boys a whole lot of freedom about when they came and went, who stayed with them, and what all went on in the room. Curfew changed every night, depending on when Bobby got sleepy. As was previously pointed out, Neenie's obesity greatly inhibited her mobility, allowing Bobby and David to live their lives free from grandmotherly intrusions. Older brother Bobby ran the show and quickly dubbed it "Club 21." It wasn't open to everyone, just to Bobby's hand-picked friends and a few of David's pals. Since I was friends with both boys, I was a charter member of Club 21.

In addition to the Wist boys and me, there were: Henry Hudson, Vernard Solomon, James Hooten, Jerry Cargill, Bailey Mosely, Joel Fagan, Danny Love, and David Mitchell. Frequent visitors included Reeves Field, John Bogue, Terry Weeks, Paul Hay, Charles Holley, and Butch Edwards. There were two things one could generally count on when he dropped by Club 21. First, there was usually a poker game going on and, secondly, music by either Bill Haley and His Comets or Roy Orbison would be blasting from the Magnavox hi-fi the Wist boys had received for Christmas.

At the risk of oversimplification, Club 21 was a poker club, a place that allowed carefully selected underaged teens to imbibe, and a group that organized and catered parties held in the homes of parents who were away for the weekend. The party-related activities were handled by a group known socially as the Big Ten, a group made up of boys who enjoyed getting together after school or on weekends for pick-up football, basketball, and/or poker games. The group was also quick to put a party together, especially at the home of someone's parents who had gone away for the weekend. The first time we staged a party in a free-for-the-weekend house, we changed all the lightbulbs from regular to blue. The blue lights gave the home a night club aura and became quite popular. For obvious reasons, they became known as "blue light parties." Our parties weren't really wild. We never "trashed" a place and always left the host home cleaner than it was before the bash. We drank a bit, played music too loud, talked, danced a little, and did some heavy-duty flirting and fooling around. Oddly enough, I don't remember any rowdiness or disorderly conduct. In fact, it would not have been tolerated.

Even though Marshall and Harrison County were "dry" back then, we were only thirty-eight miles from Shreveport-Bossier, Louisiana, where the legal drinking age was eighteen. Bossier City was just across the Red River from Shreveport, and its night club strip was easily accessed by underaged, thrill-seeking kids from East Texas. The most popular spots were Sak's Boom-Boom Room, The Stork Club, and Blue's. Blue's was on the eastern edge of the strip, and it was really more of a honky-tonk than a night club. Its crowds were a bit rougher and wilder than would be found at the other clubs. One night, we decided to "hit" Blue's, and we pulled into their parking lot. It was aglow with the flashing red lights and crackling radios of a whole slew of police cars. The entire front of the night club was ripped out as though a bomb had gone off. We later found out a thirsty fellow had driven his pulpwood truck through the front of the establishment and pulled up to the bar. The errant – though determined – driver then rolled his window down and ordered a six-pack of Jax to go. I never heard whether anyone had been hurt by the truck's intrusion or whether the brainless driver was served his six-pack. The point of telling you about Shreveport-Bossier was to let you know where we went to load up on our beer and booze, and perhaps spend some time on the wild side of life.

Of course, if we didn't have time to go to Louisiana on a beer run, we could always call on our local bootleggers. If we wanted hard liquor, we went to the home of Mr. Tucker. When he wasn't hauling timber, Tucker supplemented his income by selling half-pints of Old Crow whiskey for two dollars a bottle. If we needed beer, we went to the home of junk dealer Garfield. Garfield was a very small senior citizen who liked really big women. I know this because the back door of his house opened right into his bedroom. When we knocked on his back

Puberty Drove the Car

door and told him we needed some beer, he would crawl out of bed and come unlatch his screen door. We were then told to go to his refrigerator, get as many quarts of Falstaff beer as we needed, and leave our money on his nightstand next to his bed. Each quart was a dollar. The scene that his customers had to take in was jarring and, in my case, permanently etched in my brain. Garfield might – and I stress might – have tipped the scales at 110 pounds, but his boxer shorts hung below his knees and would easily have fit a man three times his size. When he crawled back in bed, the 300+ pounds of his girlfriend sucked him right down to her hugeness.

Louisiana, Mr. Tucker, and Garfield kept Club 21 and the Big Ten in joy juice. I guess the fact that there was alcohol available at Club 21 wasn't as big of a secret as we hoped because, late one afternoon, a highly-respected, high-ranking official of our local judicial system pulled up in front of Club 21, walked in, and asked if we would sell him a half-pint of Old Crow bourbon. We did, and he left.

Poker playing was pretty serious stuff to quite a few of us by the time we were in tenth grade. On afternoons we didn't have some sort of sports obligation, Terry Weeks, Mickey McCay, John Bogue, David Wist, and I would play poker. We didn't play for high stakes, but it was for enough to bite into a loser's dating money. Mickey and John weren't much for gambling, and neither seemed to ever fully grasp the rules for playing. Also, Mickey rarely had any money, so it was an unwritten rule that whoever won that day made certain Mickey was reimbursed any losses. Also, Terry, David, and I coached Mickey and John through each hand, exempting them from the rules. It was what you might call a "friendly" game.

Toward the end of the tenth grade, the games I participated in were for bigger stakes and were where a rule infraction became expensive. Terry and David moved up to this next league with me but shied away from the bigger stakes games. Those with whom I gambled at this level included Bobby Wist, Henry Hudson, Reeves Field, Vernard Solomon, Bobby Whelan, John Verhalen, and a few others who have slipped my mind. I had another poker group that included Ronnie McMullen, Dickie Brassell, Jerry Scott, and Al Moore. This game was a "player beware" game because it was commonly believed Ronnie, Al, and Jerry would cheat at the drop of a hat. However, because everyone watched each other so closely, it usually ended up being an honest game.

The games most frequently played were Five-card draw, Five-card stud, Five or Seven-card Mexican Sweat, Seven-card stud, High or Low Chicago, or In-Between. In most cases, the big winner would walk away from the table with fifteen to twenty-five dollars in winnings. Remember, however, we were kids, and it was the early 1960s, meaning fifteen to twenty-five dollars was quite a bit of loot. Our gambling stayed at this level until the Summer of '62 when six of us went to New Roads, Louisiana, and learned a game called "Bouree."

At the end of the 1961-1962 school year, Bobby and David Wist joined their parents in New Roads for the summer. In mid-July, Mr. and Mrs. Wist figured their boys would enjoy a visit from some Marshall friends and let each of them invite two friends to come for a couple of weeks as their guests in New Roads. Bobby invited Henry Hudson and Vernard Solomon, while David invited Terry Weeks and me. What an adventure our New Roads trip turned out to be. New Roads was a French-founded town of about four-thousand in 1962. It was the parish seat of Point Coupee Parish, located twenty-four miles West of Baton Rouge. I quickly learned this little South Louisiana town was about as friendly and hospitable as could be. I also learned that a fellow could do about anything he chose to do, including walking into any bar and drinking a beer if he was big enough to put a quarter on the bar. He could then take his beer over to a pinball machine that would pay off in real cash if he got lucky.

Bobby and David had quickly made two good friends in New Roads. Their names were Robert David (pronounced Dah-veed in cajunese), and Joe Langlois (pronounce Long-wah). Robert and Joe had taught Bobby and David a Cajun gambling card game called "Bouree" (pronounced boo-ray), and the four of them eagerly taught Henry, Vernard, Terry, and me how to play it. As all four of us visitors were seasoned poker players, we had no trouble picking up Bouree. It was easy to understand but almost impossible to control. In "no limit" Bouree, a gambler could lose his house and car before he knew what hit him. It was a heartless game that made for big winners and big losers. Fortunately, we put loss limits on our games, so suicide was off the table for most of us.

Our activities in New Roads basically centered around Bouree games and visits to one or both of our favorite watering holes. Our favorites were The Flats and Morel's Bar and Grill. Incidentally, Morel's is still in business and now operates as Morel's Seafood Restaurant. We seldom strayed from that routine until our card game was interrupted one afternoon by several local fellows asking if we could help them out of an embarrassing situation. They explained that New Roads's semi-pro baseball team was scheduled to host the team from Morgan City, Louisiana, that night and did not have enough players in town to field a team. Additionally, they had failed to line up umpires. Robert and Joe were not athletes in any sense of the word and quickly declined to help. Bobby, ever the self-appointed leader, quickly told the locals we would provide four players and the two umpires. They were elated. We, on the other hand, had three hours to shake off the effects of the few beers we had enjoyed, find baseball gloves, and psych-up for the challenge staring at us. The game was on.

Robert and Joe had come up with four gloves for us. They had no uniforms for us, although the rest of our team looked spiffy in theirs. Bobby had determined that Vernard would play in right field, Henry would play in center field, I would play shortstop, and he would pitch. That left David to be the third base umpire and Terry behind the plate to call balls and strikes. Here's a quick run-down on the player profiles of Vernard, Henry, and Bobby:

Vernard – The closest Vernard had ever been to a baseball bat was when he was holding a seven iron. He had zero athletic ability beyond golf. Bobby tried to hide Vernard in right field in hopes no one would hit a ball to him. Vernard also had no tennis shoes, so he played in his cowboy boots. Vernard hated baseball and had not shaken off the effects of the beer he had previously consumed. In short, he was snockered.

Henry – Henry had played some baseball and actually made the Little League All Stars when he was twelve years-old. He would do just fine.

Bobby – Bobby steamrolled the local team members and appointed himself team manager. As I said, he informed us he would pitch. Henry and I knew Bobby couldn't pitch worth a flip. Vernard could not have cared less. When we were warming up before the game, our catcher, a fine athlete by the name of Ahnee Jordan told Bobby he should play anywhere else but pitcher. Bobby then feigned a sore arm and told me I was going to have to pitch. He played first base and did a good job.

David – while David loved baseball and knew everything about it, base umpiring was as close as he should ever be to the game. While pitching, I picked off three opposing baserunners who were on third base. The Morgan City manager accused me of balking on all three occasions. David stuck to his guns. In reflection, I think I probably did balk on all three occasions. Thanks for your loyalty, David.

Terry – the power of being the home plate umpire quickly went to Terry's head. He wreaked of authority, although he had never played in a single organized baseball game. He was firm in his calling of balls and strikes, even when he was wrong. I think Morgan City would have given him fits if they didn't think he would throw them out of the game if they argued with him. When I was pitching, Terry would look at me before calling a pitch if he didn't know if it was a ball or a strike. If it was a ball, I would subtly shake my head. If I thought it was a strike, I would nod. Terry stood tall that night.

Scotty (me) – I was a good shortstop, but when Bobby tossed me the ball and told me I was our pitcher, I was filled with trepidation. I had been a good pitcher in Little League, but that was the last time I had toed the rubber. My uniform consisted of high-top tennis shoes, blue jeans, and a button-up madras shirt. As a tall, thin, poorly-clad 16-year-old, I hardly inspired confidence. I'm sure the opposing team took one look at me and thought, "easy pickin's." Well, much to everyone's surprise – including mine – I was anything but easy pickin's that night. In addition to pitching nine innings, I had two hits from the clean-up spot. I was a good baseball player, but not THAT good. It was just one of those nights God spilled his good grace all over me and the rag-tag baseball team from New Roads.

About forty minutes before game time, a large, air-conditioned bus pulled up to the field. As we watched the Morgan City players file off their bus, a swarm of butterflies filled our stomachs. They were grown men, some with two or three days' worth of whiskers on their faces. A number of them crammed wads of chewing tobacco into their cheeks as they looked us over. Their uniforms were crisp, and their demeanor was all business. They looked like a good baseball team. I suspect Bobby was the only guy on our team who thought we would win. Another thing happened that night to add to the electricity of the evening: the townspeople had heard about the small band of Texans who had volunteered to help New Roads defend its honor, and they showed up in droves to root us on. I was intimidated.

The Morgan City team leader was also their pitcher. He was about six foot two or three, and I'd guess he was about thirty-five years old. He wore a scowl that announced his general unhappiness to the world, and his name matched his looks and attitude. It was "Razor." On a normal night, Razor would have been a very good pitcher, but this wasn't a normal night. It was weird. It was magical. The players on both sides were right out of an Erskine Caldwell novel, but the story was Disneyesque (after a little cleaning up).

After a few innings, it became apparent that Morgan City wasn't going to bang me around the ballpark. They got a few hits, but we got more. One inning, Bobby hollered, "Vernard, you're up at bat." No Vernard. Bobby announced it louder. Still, no Vernard. Finally, someone on our team noticed the tops of Vernard's cowboy boots sticking above the uncut outfield grass in right field. Bobby raced out to investigate and found Vernard asleep in right field, using his glove as a pillow. Bobby shook Vernard to consciousness and got him to the plate for his at-bat. Razor's first pitch hit the drowsy outfielder on his left hip. Vernard just stared at him because he didn't know that if you are hit by a pitch, you are awarded first base.

When I took the mound in a middle inning, I looked around and noticed that the third base umpire, David, was smoking. Henry and Vernard were both smoking in the outfield and, most shocking of all, our home plate umpire, Terry, had a cigarette hanging out of his mask. No one complained, so I kept pitching.

The game was in the eighth inning, and we were in the field. Then, all hell broke loose. I was in the middle of a wind-up when a loud voice from the first base side of the field hollered, "HOLD IT! HOLD IT!" I, along with everyone else in the ballyard, looked around in time to see the sheriff and two deputies walking purposefully toward the pitching mound. When they reached me, they took the ball and headed to one of our players and arrested him. After they marched him off the field, the high sheriff tossed me the baseball, threw our teammate in the backseat of the cruiser, and took off. After immeasurable confusion, we all decided to complete the game. We later learned that our player, probably under the influence of Budweiser, had recently stolen all of the penny-weighing machines in town, broken into them, and then tossed them off the bridge into the False River. The sheriff and deputies had taken him straight to the bridge, handed him the end of a long rope, and told him to dive down into the dark, deep, gator and moccasin-infested water, where he was to find each scale, tie the rope around it, come up for air, and repeat the process until all of the scales had been returned to dry land. I can't remember whether the sheriff or one of his deputies was our player's uncle, but one of them was. Louisiana justice.

New Roads, Louisiana, and yours truly had enjoyed about all of the excitement we could stand for one night. Based on talent, Morgan City should have won the game easily, but they didn't. We won 11–2, and we were toasted in every bar in the little town for a week. Cajuns look for reasons to celebrate, and we had given them one. Much was made about the six Texans who saved the day for New Roads and sent Razor and his team back to Morgan City with their tails tucked between their legs. After the game, Vernard announced his retirement from baseball, Bobby hung around the field, accepting congratulations, and I accepted a fifteen dollar gift from a happy local businessman. When the lights were turned off, we all went to The Flats for a cold Bud. Thank you, Lord, for an unforgettable story with a fairytale ending.

At the end of our stay on Community Street in New Roads, we loaded into Henry's big Dodge Polara and headed back to East Texas. The Wist boys returned to Marshall a couple of weeks later, and the six of us introduced the game of Bouree to East Texas. It caught on, and a lot of money changed hands over the coming years. Soon after our return to Marshall, a few of us moved into the "serious" category of card players. We did that by moving the bouree limit from two dollars to $100.00. Without explaining the rules of bouree, let me just say that if a player elects to stay in the trick-taking hand in hopes of taking a majority of the tricks and fails to take a single trick, that player must match the amount in the pot. Failure to take a trick is called "boureeing" (boo-raying). That pot-match makes the next pot larger. After two or three pot-matches, the pot size has grown exponentially, making it very, very gutsy (or stupid) to play for the pot and risk "boo-raying." Games with an ante of only one dollar quickly raise pots in excess of $200-$300. If you are a bit confused by this cursory explanation of bouree, don't worry about it. Just trust me when I tell you it is a very high-risk and very high-reward gamble. It is not for the faint of heart.

David, Terry, John Bogue, Mickey MCay, and I continued to have our inexpensive games of bouree, but Bobby, Henry, Vernard, me, and, occasionally, David moved on to high-stakes games. Robert David and Joe Langlois came up from New Roads several times to play in the bouree games. I look back now and wonder what possessed me to play in those "big" games when only in my teens. I was a good card player and won far more than I lost. Today, it would frighten me to death to risk incurring huge losses in a game of chance. As my age has increased, my nerve has decreased. Could that change have been caused by the onset of wisdom? Surely not.

The Bob Hope Motel, which had been such a big part of my life in 1961 and 1962, sold in the Summer of '62. Neenie's age and poor health necessitated her freeing herself from the work and worries associated with running a business. She sold it to her brother-in-law, O. C. Hope, who was a larger-than-life local businessman. Mr. Hope was a cattleman, an oilman, a land and buildings owner, and an unbridled entrepreneur. Some of his own family members referred to him years after his prime as Marshall's version of "Boss" Hogg, the man who ran Hazzard County in the television series, *The Dukes of Hazzard*. Mr. Hope was a long-standing good friend to my family, so it surprised no one when he hired me to be his night clerk during the summer and clerk on weekends during the school year. I worked for Mr. Hope for two years until I went away to college. During that time, I became a great admirer of his and treasured our evening talks around the huge fireplace he added to the motel's lobby. As an aside, my oldest brother, Homer, had worked a summer or two for Neenie while he was a college student, so I was the second Eubanks boy to be paid by a Hope.

The Hopes were integral parts of Marshall and Harrison County's history. The old Hope home sat near Caddo Lake and was a prominent county landmark. Mr. Hope once showed me a photo of the house and pointed out the window of the bedroom where the outlaw Frank James slept during his occasional visits with Mr. Hope's dad, Oscar Hope. Mr. Hope remembered Frank's visits and remembered his dad and Frank sitting on the front porch talking after supper. Mr. Hope regaled me with stories about the times I had studied in history class. To me, he was living history.

When Neenie sold the motel to Mr. Hope, it meant Club 21 and the Big 10 and its blue light parties ceased to be. In the fall, eight of the Big 10 went away to college, leaving only Henry and me behind to finish high school. It was a summer of change, and while we would often yearn for those "good old days," they were soon replaced by new ways to stretch the boundaries of propriety.

By being the night clerk at the Bob Hope Motel, I learned that many of the truckers, salesmen, and other motel guests were road-weary when they checked in and asked where they could get some cold beer or a cocktail. They were most unhappy when I reminded them our city and county were dry, meaning alcohol sales of any kind were against the law. A plan hatched. I started buying a half pint or two of

Old Crow from Mr. Tucker and six or eight quarts of Falstaff from Garfield to keep on hand for thirsty travelers. The Coke machine that was in our lobby had a large storage area in its bottom for the storage of extra soft drinks. I used it to store Falstaffs instead, and I hid the Old Crow in the linen closet. I sold the half-pints for three dollars and the quarts of beer for two dollars, netting a dollar on each sale. The thought of being arrested for bootlegging never crossed my mind. Stupid. Highly profitable, but stupid.

My last day of work at Bob Hope Motel, a day or two before I went off to Stephen F. Austin University, Mr. Hope asked to borrow my car. He had never done that before, but I tossed him my keys and continued to work. About two hours later, he returned to the motel and parked my 1955 Ford. He brought me my keys and went about his business. When I had finished my work, he walked with me to my car, and we said our good-byes with a firm handshake and an awkward hug. As I was about to get into my car, I noticed my left, rear tire looked new. I slowly walked around my car and noticed I had four brand-new tires. I questioningly looked at Mr. Hope, and he just shyly smiled and told me to drive carefully. When I started my car, I saw I had a full tank of gas. I loved that old man.

The Bob Hope Motel was torn down many years ago and was replaced by other commercial ventures, but every time I ride by that site, I only see the storied motel. It was a big part of my life for several of my most impressionable years, as were the Wist boys, their grandmother Neenie, Club 21 members, the Big 10, Mr. O. C. Hope and his family.

Neenie Hope, grandmother of Bobby and David Wist.

Chapter 17

TV, Elvis, Hairspray, and English Leather

By now, you realize my writing has been fueled by my great memories and a near epidemic case of nostalgia. There are many difficult tasks to be accomplished in writing any book, including a book that heavily relies on nostalgia for content. One of the things I struggled with was how to handle the fads, fashions, music, movies, etc. that helped define the late 1950s and early 1960s. To just start seeding these things into my many stories seemed a tad contrived and would have added no value to them. Instead, I opted to write a little bit about them and, in some cases, to simply list them. Handling these hallmarks of our era in this manner will enable the reader to run through his memory bank for the stories that were part of his teen years. Take your time, and recall the good stuff.

By the end of the 1950s, television had pretty much claimed evenings in the American home. *I Love Lucy* and *The Red Skelton Show* put a smile on our nation's face, *The Ed Sullivan Show* entertained us, and Marshall Matt Dillon kept our streets free of bad guys. Women cottoned to Liberace and Lawrence Welk while the men got their adrenalin highs from watching the *Wednesday Night Fights*, the *Friday Night Fights*, and NFL football on Sunday afternoons. In the 1960s, Perry Mason showed us there really were some honest, intelligent lawyers, Brett Maverick charmed his way into our hearts, and Rod Serling's *Twilight Zone* proved to us that our siblings weren't the only weird people on our planet. Alfred Hitchcock? Well, he just kept us off balance and a wee bit on edge.

Almost unnoticed by most families, television began to move people away from their dining rooms and into their dens, and it relentlessly chipped away at the old family tradition of conversing together. Comparing one's self or one's family to those seen on television began to cause dissatisfaction among some and caused others to wonder why their families couldn't be like Beaver's or Donna Reed's. It seemed like television was on a secret mission to generate discordant ripples in America, and it was off to a good start. I knew trouble was brewing for our young people when our bike rides and ballgames started getting interrupted by kids wanting to watch *The Howdy Doody Show*, *Sky King*, or *The Mickey Mouse Club*. Many kids started going outside only when there was nothing they wanted to watch on TV. Television's uses of fantasies and improbabilities moved some of America's constant viewers a few steps farther away from reality. Also, the medium's overuse of beautiful women and handsome men made it tough on average-to-ugly looking folks. When the networks did use anyone but great lookers, they were usually cast as villains, failures, wackos, buffoons, or other unsavory characters.

Television has become enormously influential in determining what we think, how we act, how we live, and what we do or don't do. It is incredibly powerful. Personally, I would feel better about it if it was headquartered in Iowa versus California. I think there is still a modicum of common sense in Iowa. I do not feel that way about California. I am in awe of television, and I rank its invention right up there with fire, the wheel, the automobile, the computer, and crème brûlée as the most important inventions of man.

The late '50s and early '60s also witnessed some radical changes in the American music scene. Superstars like Frank Sinatra, Doris Day, Dean Martin, Hank Williams, and Patti Page yielded much of their spotlight to newbies like Elvis, Ray Charles, Chuck Berry, Rick Nelson, and Connie Francis. Buddy Holly, Paul Anka, and Frankie Avalon caused teenaged girls to swoon, while Aretha Franklin, Marvin Gaye, The Coasters, and The Supremes led the Motown Sound to the forefront of popularity. Johnny Cash developed a bit of a cult following with his deep, mournful voice that gave audiences glimpses into the hard life he had lived. Roy Orbison was so different in sound and looks that teens loved him.

That same time period also saw silly, whimsical songs pop up and take-off in popularity. See if you can recall any of the following. If you can, I've got a pretty good idea as to how old you are. "Purple People Eater," "Alley Oop," "The Monster Mash," "Mr. Custer," "Itsy Bitsy Teenie Weenie Yellow Polka Dot Bikini," "Tie Me Kangaroo Down," "Beep Beep," "Ahab, the Arab," "Does Your Chewing Gum Lose Its

Flavor," and "My Boomerang Won't Come Back." If you are in my age group, I'll bet you not only remember these songs, but can still sing most of their words. Right?

Everyone has to make his own lists of favorites from his youth. It is truly a subjective exercise, but one guaranteed to put a smile on the list maker's face. My guess is that each generation of teenagers has juked, jived, and flipped-out to music unique to the tastes of their time. Our generation of jive-monkeys had the unique privilege of watching rock-and-roll sweep the world and the British Invasion – led by the Beatles – change our tastes in both music and boys' hairstyles. We watched Elvis use gyrating, swiveling hips and a curved lip to cause young women to swoon and sometimes faint. When I tried to gyrate like Elvis, I looked as though I had stuck my finger in the electrical outlet.

While previous generations danced their Charlestons, Lindy Hops, and Swings, we tried new dances on a regular basis. The Jitterbug was the mainstay for our fast dancing, but more dances became short-lived fads than you could shake a stick at. In the late 1950s, we did the Bop, the Bunny Hop, and the Stroll. If you and your date had attended Mrs. Cowley's Dance School, you would occasionally break-out into the Cha Cha or the Bosa Nova. One dance that came along proved to be more than a fad was the Twist. Chubby Checker was the undisputed Twist master, and his song, "The Twist," along with Joey Dee and the Starliters' hit, "The Peppermint Twist," took the nation by storm. Doing the Twist was so popular with young people, the medical industry warned that "twisting" was dangerous to the joints and ligaments of the dancers. No one heeded the warnings, and we all twisted right through our high school years without injury

Some of the fad dances that enjoyed their 15 minutes of fame in the early 1960s were The Frug, The Loco-motion, The Chicken, The Swim,• The Mashed Potato, The Watusi, The Bristol Stomp, and The Pony.

I may not have done these dances well, but I do recall trying to do each of them. By the way, I thought about titling this book *I Wanted to Frug, but She Just Kept on Twisting*. I chickened out because of the obvious innuendo.

In this section dealing with songs and dances, I've more-or-less skipped right over slow-dance songs and how we danced to them. Make no mistake, we did listen and dance to slow music. Slow-dancing was crucial for two reasons. First, after doing four or five straight heart-pounding fast dances in a row, we needed a chance to slow down and catch our breaths. Second, slow dancing was legalized hugging with your partner. Singers like Johnny Mathis, Tommy Edwards, and Andy Williams incited tons of hugging.

One time when I was in the seventh grade, I met my girlfriend, Carol Marshal, at our teen center, the Marshall Corral Club. We were both recent graduates of Mrs. Cowley's Dance School, so we jitterbugged to fast songs and box waltzed to the slow ones. I was happy enough, but during a break, the prettiest girl in the Western Hemisphere, Annabelle Holcomb, asked me to slow dance with her. Annabelle was a ninth-grader and had already achieved superstar status as a beauty. Why me? She could have danced with anyone in Marshall. Again, why me? I was as nervous as a mosquito in a jar of DDT. She was so relaxed and gracious. I was in a state of body lock-down and sweated profusely. I was so nervous, I couldn't enjoy my moment of ecstasy. When the dance was over, she thanked me for the dance. I thanked her back, then went to the boy's room where I practiced deep breathing until my equilibrium returned. The rest of the evening, I strutted around the Corral like Barney Fyffe with a gun full of bullets. Annabelle, I don't know if you asked me to dance because you were Carol's friend, took pity on a lowly seventh-grader, or just found me wildly attractive, but thank you for making my night. See, I still haven't forgotten it.

Before I leave the subject of dancing, I have a confession to make. About fifteen years ago, some hot music came on television, and I jumped off the sofa and started cutting a rug. I held out my hand to my wife, Kay, inviting her to dance with me. She declined, but I kept right on dancing, convinced I was impressing her no end. After the dance, I asked Kay why she had turned me down, feigning hurt feelings as I did so. In her always-calm voice, she patted the sofa next to her, signaling me to sit down. She gently took my hand, looked me in the eyes, and told me, "Scott, I love you dearly and have for many years. However, it's time someone told you the truth about your fast-dancing. You are not only a bad fast-dancer, but you may very well be the worst fast-dancer that ever missed a beat." I had spent all those years thinking I was the cat's meow when fast-dancing only to find out I was living a lie. I felt as though I needed to send a note of apology to all those young women I had slung and drug around the dance floor for oh-so-long. I'm stilled bummed.

While I'm tempted to get into a discussion about the movies and

Hollywood stars of the '50s and '60s, I won't. Movie studios successfully deified scads of movie stars – too many to just name a few. Like with the American automobiles, small towns, and major league baseball, the '50s and '60s represented the peak years of Hollywood's success and popularity. People from generations other than mine can argue their generations enjoyed the best Hollywood had to offer, but I'm locked into mine. Save your breath.

Since I have been trying to capture the sights and sounds we experienced while growing up in the 1950s and 1960s, I might as well take a shot at capturing the scents we smelled. I'm not talking about the scents of skunks, cow paddies, and cabbage cooking. I'm talking about the fragrances girls and boys wore to maximize their allure to the opposite sex. Girls sprayed, dabbed, and splashed their perfumes in some weird places. I understood why they put it on their necks or behind their ears. Those places matched-up nicely to a boy's nose if they were cuddling or dancing. However, it strained me to figure out why some girls splashed a bit on their wrists, a dab in the fold of their arm or behind their knees. Even today, I figure a female would think I was loony if I dove in and started kissing in the bend of their arm or on her wrists. I, also, figure she would knock the thunder out of me if I went to the floor and started nuzzling the backs of her knees. If she didn't want action in those spots, why did she bait the areas?

When it came to choosing a product for improving one's smell, I think men had an easier time than women in making their selection. Men only had to choose between aftershave and cologne. Women, on the other hand, had to choose between perfume, parfum, cologne, eau de cologne, and eau de toilette (toilet water). That eau de toilette thing has always thrown me for a loop. Fragrance companies have long been leaders in image advertising. Through the years, they have convinced lots of females they could look like Liz Taylor, Katherine Deneuve, Julia Roberts, or Angelina Jolie just by smelling like them. The truth is, an unattractive person who smells good is just that: an unattractive person who smells good. Same principle holds for men, too. I could bathe in cologne, and I still wouldn't rival Johnny Depp, Jake Gyllenhaal, or Brad Pitt when it came to being cool, sexy, and handsome. However, while acknowledging the marketing genius of these fragrance companies, I have to ask a question of them. Why the hell did you ever come up with "eau de toilette?" The moment of inspiration that gave birth to that term was just plain dumb. Dumb, dumb, dumb. Can you imagine the female of your dreams bragging to you that she had doused herself with her finest toilet water? Yuck!

During my junior and senior high school years, the female fragrances I recall were Estee Lauder, Woodhue, Youth Dew, and Evening in Paris. I know there were many other fragrances for girls, but those are the ones I remember. I also remember dating someone who wore White Shoulders. I can't remember the girl, but I can't forget the wonderful aroma. Loved it.

A search of my memory came up with the following aftershaves and colognes for boys: Old Spice, Brut, Aqua Velva, English Leather, British Sterling, Aramis, Jade East, Hai Karate, Bay Rum, and Musk Oil.

I think I used English Leather, Aramis, and British Sterling. One of my closest friends was a Brut devotee. Another close friend sold out to Jade East. Like most of us at that age, they used far too much of it. When over-dousers were in the car with us, we had to roll all the windows down to neutralize the assault on our senses and, in some cases, to keep from throwing up. It worked out okay, though, because boys didn't dance with boys in those days.

Women's hairspray was quite prevalent when I was in high school. A girl needed lots of spray net (a term invented by Helene Curtis in 1950) to secure their bouffants, beehives, and other teased and ratted hairstyles. Though not invented until 1950, hair spray products like Spray Net, Aqua Net, and Hidden Magic became so popular that in 1964, hair spray outsold lipstick. Go figure.

Men's hair products were pretty basic. If you had a flat-top, you needed Butch Wax and a special round plastic brush. A crew cut needed nothing. It was virtually maintenance-free. If your hair was long enough to part, your selection for hair applications was generally limited to Vaseline Hair Tonic, Brylcream, Vitalis, Pomade, or Wildroot Cream Oil.

Vitalis was so high in alcohol content, you could put it on your hair, light it, and watch it burn off without damaging your hair. When I was in the Merchant Marines, workers shipping out on a cruise could only take one or two-fifths of whiskey with them on a trip that often lasted 3-6 months. Seamen who were confirmed drinkers used to carry lots of Aqua Velva with them, claiming it had enough alcohol in it to get them through their rough times. If I had been smarter back then, I would have sold them lots of Vitalis to go with their Aqua Velva.

Chapter 18

A Hodgepodge of Unrelated Stories

In writing a memoir, the author generally ends up with memories of unusual happenings and people who don't fit into any particular chapter. I have a handful of such vignettes that need to be told. I realize it's a bit unorthodox to write a chapter that offers no continuity of thought, but Kurt Vonnegut made a great living by confusing his readers with random thoughts that often went in all directions at the same time, so maybe this hodgepodge of stories will prove entertaining.

THE BURNING BEAST

Bailey Moseley has always been very likable. In high school, he was also muscled up like King Kong and was darn near as hairy. Because of his strength and hairiness, his friends affectionately called him "Beast." One afternoon, Bobby Wist, Paul Hay, and I stopped by his house to pick him up before heading out to do whatever we were going to do. Mrs. Mosely let us in and told us Bailey was getting dressed, and we should just go on back to the bedroom he shared with brothers Haywood and Sam. Bailey, clad in shorts and a madras shirt, was sitting on the edge of his bed pulling on his white crew socks.

When his socks were on, Bailey decided to amuse us by showing us a new trick he had just heard about. He had learned that you could light your white sock, and the fuzz on it would flame up and quickly burn the outer layer of fuzz off without harming it. To demonstrate, Beast borrowed Bobby's Zippo and lit his sock. As promised, his sock caught fire and quickly burned all of the fuzz off of his sock. Unfortunately, the fire rapidly jumped from his sock to his hairy leg. His sock fire fizzled out, but the fire on his leg hair was quickly working its way toward his knee when panic set in. Bailey, with Bobby's help, was able to beat the flames into submission before they spread to his upper body. The burning hair smelled so bad, we insisted Bailey wash his leg with soap before starting on our nightly rounds. Neat trick, Bailey.

A MISMATCH OF MIGHT

Hands down, one of the toughest kids in high school was Ronnie McMullen. He was built like a wood-splitting wedge, wide at the shoulders and narrow at the hips. He was fearless, fast as greased lightning, and powerful enough to do you some harm. One day, Ronnie decided he was mad at one of the Schuler twins, Stanley or Stephen (I can't remember which one), so, as was his custom, he waited for Schuler after school to beat him up. This match-up made no sense to anyone because Ronnie was a smart boy, and both of the Schuler twins were easygoing and harmless.

I figured Ronnie was smart enough to remember that as tough as he was, he was 5'2" tall and weighed maybe 120 pounds. The guy he was picking on was well over six feet tall and weighed in excess of 250 pounds. I figured Ronnie could discern that the numbers just didn't add up in his favor. He must have had a brain full of stupid that afternoon because he was bound and determined to whip Schuler's butt. Schuler tried to walk away from the fight and avoid the conflict. Despite Schuler's reticence to fight, Ronnie threw a punch at Schuler that didn't even phase the gentle giant. Schuler retaliated with one blow to Ronnie's face that put him out cold on the ground. Fight over. Schuler didn't stand around gloating. He just went on his way. When Ronnie came to, he discovered he wasn't nearly as mad at the Schuler twin as he had thought he was.

I once heard a joke that said the height of ambition was an ant crawling up an elephant's leg with rape on his mind. Well, that day at Marshall High, the height of ambition was Ronnie McMullen trying to go toe-to-toe with a Schuler twin. Here's the lesson I learned that day: if your enemy can put you in his pocket, retreat.

THE DAY TOM DOOLEY PASSED THROUGH MARSHALL

As I've mentioned numerous times, a favorite pastime for Marshall teens was to cruise up and down Grand Avenue to see who you could hook-up with and to just be seen. During one such outing, I parked my '55 Ford on Grand near the intersection of Grand and North Washington Street. I then jumped in John Bogue's car to ride around with him. Terry Weeks and Mickey McCay also joined us. I was riding shotgun. After about an hour of aimless cruising, we pulled up at the stoplight at the intersection of Grand and Alamo. In a short time, a fellow pulled up next to us in the lane to our right. I told the gang that the guy to our right had a car just like mine.

When the light turned green, we all pulled away, and I really looked the car over. It not only looked like mine, it was mine. We pulled even with the man, and I asked him if that was his car. He said it wasn't, and he asked me if it was my car. I said it was. He nodded and said he would pull over, which he did. He and I got out of our cars; he handed me my keys and calmly informed me that I had a nice car. I thanked him and asked him to get in the back seat of John's Ford. He did, and we found out he was driving my car to Shreveport, Louisiana, where he planned to leave it "for me." Reckon?

When I looked at his driver's license, I noticed his name was Tom Dooley. Since it had only been a couple of years since The Kingston Trio had their song, "Hang Down Your Head Tom Dooley," hit number one on the record charts, it was all we could do to keep from laughing out loud. At this point, I couldn't resist looking at him and singing the words, "Hang down your head Tom Dooley, you're about to go to jail." We did take Tom to jail, but I didn't press charges. He had been such a gentleman in our odd encounter that I didn't want to add to his obvious woes. He spent the night in a cell and, the next morning, Officer Wallace dropped him off on U.S. 80, so he could continue on his way to Shreveport. After that, I quit leaving my keys in the car.

A HEARD OF WORMS AT MARSHALL HIGH

In 1962, our Marshall Maverick football team compiled a record of three wins, six losses, and one tie (3–6–1). It had been an up and down season but one slightly bruised by friction between some of the players and many of the male students who did not play football. I suppose in an effort to build team spirit and pride in being on the football team, two or three of the assistant coaches began telling the footballers they were the elite of MHS and should only run around with each other. These same two or three coaches started referring to all non-football players as "worms," and the players were told that the worms weren't worthy of their attention. At this point, I want to make it clear that all of our coaches were dedicated to their jobs and doing it the way they thought best. I also want to stress the fact that only two or three of them spearheaded the separatist movement that led to a rift between players and non-players.

Some of the footballers who were highly impressionable looked up to their coaches so much and were so gung-ho that they completely bought into the bad advice preached to them by the coaches. They avoided the worms like the plague and often made their disdain clear when in their presence. Longstanding friendships fell apart over the issue, and while not all of the football players took the coaches' bait, enough did so to cause a major squabble within the halls of MHS. It soon became a badge of honor to be a worm. The offending couple of coaches were relentless in their bullying and degrading of the "worms." I personally think our head coach, Dub Wooten, was somewhat oblivious to the harm his underlings did to school morale. Truthfully, I liked him and thought him to be a man of high character. Those of us who played other sports for the Mavericks were generally immune to the "worm" tag, but if I had been forced to choose which side I stood with, I would have easily chosen the worms. They had done nothing to deserve the demeaning attention cast upon them by the misguided coaches.

Many fine athletes sat out of organized sports because of the animosity they felt for certain members of the football coaching staff. This group of boys, joined by other athletic worms, used to meet at the baseball field after school to play tackle football without the protection of helmets and pads. I played in many of these games and, believe me when I tell you, these were well-played, tough games. It was blatantly obvious that the Mavericks had missed out on lots and lots of football talent. The outfield area of the field became known as "Worm Stadium," and the games grew to draw minor crowds.

The next year, the primary coaches who had engineered the worm controversy moved on, so the worm-versus-footballers friction cooled considerably. One holdover coach tried to keep the denigration of non-football players alive, but he didn't have an audience.

During our senior year, 1964, only five senior boys went out for football, an alarmingly low number for a large high school in football-crazy Texas. Of the five, only three made the starting team. The three starters were D. H. Martin, Palmer Pratt, and Roy Lee Fry. They were the best three football players in our class, and that would not have changed even if all the boys in our class had played for the Mavericks. They all won scholarships to major universities, and they deserved them. This low turnout of seniors was unheard of in Texas high school football. We had well over 320 students in our senior class, so it was safe to assume about half of those were boys. It's further safe to assume more than three of those boys were talented enough to be quality Maverick starters. D. H., Palmer, and Roy Lee deserved to share the field with the other good athletes of their class. Too bad.

Many of us who skipped football lost interest in playing because of the worm controversy. Clearly, we all supported the team and our fellow-seniors who played on it, and our informal boycott was aimed at the coaches, not our classmates. Our team went winless our senior year. It shouldn't have.

MY DATE WAS ON FIRE!

When I was a freshman in college, I started dating a high school senior named Kay Hightower. I would come home on weekends for dates and to accompany her to her senior parties. Early in our courtship, there was a dress-up dance for the seniors held at the Marshall Country Club. Kay looked absolutely stunning, and I couldn't wait to get to the country club to show her off. For this special occasion, she had rolled her hair into tiny curls secured high on top of her head by invisible bobby pins and tons of hairspray to hold them in place. It looked great.

Our romantic evening took a weird turn when she bent over to sign our names in the registration book. In the process, her stack of hair came in contact with a candle that adorned the sign-in table. The hairspray caught on fire and flamed up as it ate into her blond hair. A couple of other girls joined her in beating out the flame. She and her friends went off to the ladies' room for damage control. They did an admirable job, and we had a wonderful night of dancing. The only problem I had – and it was a big one – was that when we slow danced, my nose fit right into the hole in her hair the fire had caused. Boy, did it stink! The burnt hair smelled so bad my eyes kept watering. That was the first, and only, time I ever had a date break out in flames. Oh, by the way, Kay and I have now been married more than fifty-three years, so the flame is proving to be eternal.

WAS IT A STRIKE OR A STRIKEOUT? NO. IT WAS A SPLIT

On another one of my early dates with Kay Hightower, we went bowling. It was still early in our blossoming relationship, so I was doing my best to impress her. I wore a brand-new pair of white shorts, thinking they would show off the tan on my skinny legs. I thought I looked good and was just short of strutting. We got our rental shoes, picked out our bowling balls, and settled in on lane #3. She went first.

When I stepped-up to bowl, I focused on looking cool and doing well. When I bent over to release my first ball of the day, my new shorts ripped from the beltline around and under to the zipper. It wasn't a small rip. It was a full-throttle rip complete with sound effects. My first reaction was to quickly pray that I had not worn any of my holey underwear. Kay was rolling with laughter while I was bright red with embarrassment. With the bowling alley's permission, we ran to my house for a change of shorts and a check to make certain I was wearing good underwear. I was. We returned to finish our bowling. We didn't set any bowling records that day, but we created a memory we still laugh about. I got a full refund on the white shorts.

MRS. HUGHES WAS TIPSY? OH, COME ON!

David Wist tells the story about a classroom Christmas party that got out of hand in Inez Hughes's classroom in 1962. It was the last day of classes before the Christmas holidays, and Mrs. Hughes decided to serve cookies and punch to all her students throughout the day. During first period, David says he laced the punch with a generous splash of white lightning he got from his brother, Bobby. Ever in the Christmas spirit, Mrs. Hughes enjoyed at least one cup of "hard" punch with each of her classes. David says that by the end of the day, Mrs. Hughes was as loose as a goose and ready to party down. You'll note that I credit this story to David. I do so because I have trouble imagining Inez Hughes out-of-control to any degree, at any time. If it's not true, it's on you, David.

IS HE DRINKING FROM HIS NOTEBOOK, OR IS HE JUST NUTS?

For seniors, the last week of school was anything but rigid in terms of rules enforcement. Most of us had strong enough grades to be exempt from final exams. Lots of kids cut classes during this time, and others found different ways to fritter away the time until graduation. One friend of mine put his hand-tooled zip-up leather notebook to a use for which it was never intended. In study hall, he carefully placed a half-pint of peach brandy inside his notebook and positioned it to where the top of the bottle protruded slightly from the zipped-up notebook. He could then place a hand on each side of the notebook to hold the bottle firmly in place, lift it to where the bottle's lip met his lips, and enjoy slugs of his peach brandy. No one ever called his hand on it, but I wonder if it crossed his mind how stupid he looked, holding his notebook against his face over and over again.

A CASE OF BAD TIMING

I had many jobs as a teenager. One of those summer jobs was at Smith's Furniture in Downtown Marshall. After I was hired, I was told I could pick a friend to come work with me. I selected David Wist. The two of us were delivery boys, inventory movers, dusters, assemblers, carpet layers, and doers of a whole host of odd jobs no one else wanted to do. Much of the unshown merchandise was kept in a somewhat dank basement that could only be reached via an old hand-drawn freight elevator. Between chores, David and I would hang out down there, figuring that staying out-of-sight was a smart move. David suffered from a yet-to-be diagnosed case of narcolepsy, so he usually curled up on a stored mattress for a nap.

One afternoon, I was exploring while David slept, and I found a spot where one could walk out an old window into an area below the sidewalk above and look up through a metal grate into the fresh air. I quickly realized this vantage point afforded a look right up the skirt of any female that walked over it on the busy sidewalk. In my excitement to share the discovery with my good friend, I woke David up so he could check it out. Still half asleep, David took up a position under the grate just as a beat cop stopped on it and spit a loogie down through the grate. The mass of mucus hit David right between the eyes. Ooh, bad timing, partner. That incident stopped us from ever checking out the action on the other side of the metal grate. From then on, I just read while David slept.

CALHOUN'S REBELLION

Every high school has its characters. Ours was a fellow named James Calhoun. I can't swear to it, but I think James quit school the first day it became legal. With that in mind, I don't think he was a student when he pulled the prank I'm about to share with you. Anyone who knew James knew he was a real cut-up and not focused on making the honor roll. All that aside, order in the classrooms of MHS was shattered one afternoon by the incredibly loud sound of an unmuffled engine echoing through the hallowed halls of our three-story high school. Many of us overran our teachers to fill the hallways in search of the source of the roaring sound. It turns out that James had somehow managed to get his unmufflered motor scooter up the three flights of stairs and was now riding it through the halls and, ultimately, down the stairs at the other end of the building. Even though the stairs were jarring his teeth mercilessly, he never lost his big smile. I strongly believe James had long dreamed of making such a ride and that this bodacious ride was a fantasy fulfilled. Way to go, James. You won the day.

UNDER THE SPELL OF "THE BLACK CAT"

I am sure you noticed along life's way that some boys had "street smarts" long before others their age did. I was one of those kids. Now, don't misunderstand me, there were other boys who were farther along on the street savvy scale than I was, but I was well ahead of most. There were lots of kids smarter than me and many kids more street-wise. However, at the risk of shamelessly patting myself on the back, I say very few kids combined those assets as well as I did.

I think having brothers who were ten and thirteen years older than me, both of whom were rounders, got me off to an early start toward developing street smarts. Each of them got into enough binds and predicaments to write a couple of chapters in my book on developing street sense. Our dad must have invented street smarts because he never ceased to amaze us with his earthy wisdom and uncommon understanding of human nature. He had seen it all, and he had done it all. Plus, he was hellbent on teaching his three boys how to survive in any environment. Mother may have coddled us a bit, but daddy didn't at all.

Regardless of the influences that got me to my point of street savvy, I knew how to play poker, shoot craps, shoot pool, throw a knife, and do other things by the time I was twelve. I also knew how to get along with folks from all different backgrounds and interests. I was comfortable in about any situation in which I found myself.

While I credit Daddy, my brothers, and my older friends with much of my street education, there's another fellow who deserves a doff of my hat. That man is my dearly-departed Uncle Blackie. Blackie was my mother's younger brother and half of a twin set that included Uncle Whitey. As the name implies, Blackie had black hair, and Whitey was blonde. Whitey was a day person. Blackie was a night person. Blackie ran my grandparents bar in Alexandria, Louisiana, from 4 p.m. to 1 a.m., seven days a week for countless years. This lifestyle wasn't conducive to a good marriage, so Blackie was divorced and separated from his two kids for much of their lives. He lived a lonesome life and, since he slept most of the daylight hours, he did most of his living after midnight. Because of his nocturnal existence, everyone referred to him as "Black Cat." The fact that he wore dark prescription sunglasses day and night added to his black cat image.

From the time I was twelve on through my teens, I would spend two to three weeks with my grandparents in Alexandria. They liked to go to bed very early, so I would hang out in the bar with Uncle Blackie. I was serving beer in the bar by the time I was twelve, which exposed me to lots of "earthy" happenings. During free minutes, Blackie showed me how to play a mean game of electronic shuffleboard, a skill with which I won quite a lot of money from bar patrons. The more they drank, the more I won. He also taught me how to throw darts very well, a game from which I also profited. The Black Cat was a master at bar games and generously cut me in on his action.

When Blackie closed up around one in the morning, he wasn't always ready for bed. Often, we would go bowling, but sometimes we went to the honky-tonks in the river bottom where closing time was determined by when the action died down. Most of these honky-tonks were built on stilts because the river often flooded. Let me be clear that these were not night clubs or family bars. They were hardcore dives that attracted a clientele that was at home in "diveland." Blackie was well-known and well-liked by all the patrons and, because of his popularity, I was tolerated. By the time I was 14, I knew how to honky-tonk dance and a few other "dark side" things I couldn't tell Mother about. One night in such a bar, I won several dollars in an icepick throwing competition. Did I mention earlier that Uncle Blackie had taught me how to throw an icepick. In many Louisiana bars that didn't have a dartboard, ice pick throwing was a popular pastime.

When I was sixteen or seventeen, my friend John Bogue went with me to Alexandria. He got to experience several nights in the river bottom with the Black Cat for himself. On those occasions, if John and I sat still too long, Uncle Blackie would send a couple of what my grandmother called "floozies" over to dance with us. Uncle Blackie was a very thoughtful man who often enriched my life, even though he always called me "Iron Head." He taught me how to shoot pool, taught me all about how to put different spins (called "English" in the lingo) on the cue ball, playing each shot in such a way to set up the next shot (called "leave"), and how to break in a way to maximize your chance at sinking a ball in the side pocket. Thanks to Blackie, I got good at pool, but I never could beat Ronnie McMullen. I guess he had an Uncle Blackie, too

Chapter 19

And Then It Was Over

Now what?

In May of 1964, my six years of junior and senior high school ended with a Charlie Flowers speech at our graduation ceremony, held at Maverick Stadium. The moment after our last graduating senior, Barbara Young, walked across the stage and received her diploma, Maverick Stadium erupted with the sounds of joy and celebration that accompanied similar ceremonies all over the country. There were cries of joy, congratulatory hugs, whoopin' and hollerin', and a silent – but palpable – collective sigh of relief. For some, it meant school was over in their lives, and they could get on about the business of living. For others, it meant they were off to college for new adventures in learning and in life. For all, it meant a new freedom they had earned.

Post-graduation optimism ruled the day. News about who was going to college where, which high school lovers were getting married, which relationships were breaking up, who was going to major in what subject, and other topics pertaining to our future were what we all talked about. We knew we had made a giant step toward adulthood, and we embraced the chance to move on down that road. It was a time for us to see the good things that lay ahead for us and not even ponder the bad. We were happy.

A few weeks after graduation, the many changes I was about to face began to dawn on me. While I was truly upbeat about going off to college, I began to suffer a little bit of post-partum anxiety. I also struggled a bit with the realization that the kids with whom I had been raised were about to scatter in many different directions. Lastly, I had trouble dealing with moving away from home, leaving my mother to an empty house. My dad had died my junior year in high school, and Mother and I developed a solid dependency on each other. My two older brothers did a great job of watching over Mother, but they had family responsibilities of their own. Suffice it to say, leaving Mother was tough on me. Don't get me wrong. Happiness, optimism, and enthusiasm were my primary feelings, but I knew the life I was stepping away from had been blessed and darn near idyllic.

By August of that summer, I knew where most of my friends were going to college. Lynn Abney chose Oklahoma University, Nancy Brown was headed to Southern Methodist University, David Wist enrolled at Texas, John Bogue went to Kilgore, Carol Marshall became a Baylor Bear, and a whole slew of us went to Stephen F. Austin State University (SFA) in Nacogdoches, Texas. My best pal, Terry Weeks, and I managed to be roommates. Other close friends who enrolled at SFA were Frank Timmins, Charlie Starke, Tuck Kemper, Will DuShane, David Applebaum, Mickey McCay, Mike Briggs, Glenn Thomas, and a healthy number of girls and other friends from Marshall High School. I was also thrilled to be re-joining my long-time friend Dick Cole who was already attending SFA. Having so many friends around went a long way toward weaning me from my dependency on Marshall, Mother, and my friends who went different directions after graduation.

I won't write any more memoirs, but if I did, I would concentrate on trying to capture the sense of excitement I felt about what my future had in store for me. I would also reflect on the varied roads my good friends chose to follow as they put their college years in their rearview mirrors. I have carefully followed the lives of my friends. I've shared in their successes, shared their pains, and grieved over their deaths. Despite all of the bumps in the road we have all faced in our lives, I will always remember my friends with the smiles of joy, optimism, strength, and goodness that were ever-etched across their faces.

The ties of friendship made in those early years of growing up in Marshall, Texas, will forever remain unbroken by miles, time, and old age. My memories are great; my friendships are even greater.

The author Louis L'Amour once wrote, "There will come a time when you believe everything is finished. That will be the beginning." It was our beginning.

Acknowledgments

If a writer tells you he didn't have help writing his book, he's either a fibber, or his book is lousy. I'm going to tell you who helped me write *Puberty Drove the Car, I Was Just Along for the Ride*, so if you don't enjoy it, I can share the blame with them.

I had editing help from Kim Matthews; Henry Croom; my daughter, Mary Bratz; my son, Paul Eubanks; and my wife, Kay, who – like she's done throughout our longstanding marriage – offered much sage advice and helped me avoid lots of mistakes. She was outstanding at helping me maintain my focus, often re-aiming me when I strayed into the literary unknown. At times, I thought Kay found an inordinate amount of joy in finding my mistakes, but maybe I was just being overly sensitive. You rock, Kato.

On the research side, I leaned heavily on old friends and former classmates Leslie Lawrence, Jerry Foley, Dick Cole, Jerry Cargill, and Wayne Bogue for help in writing about the cars of our era. Francene Neely Lewis and David Ponder were invaluable to me as I wrote my chapter on Neely's Drive-In. My seventh-grade teacher, Lucile Estell, coached me on Marshall's history. Diane Whitis Reed helped me with my junior high memories, and David Wist supplemented my memories with his versions of the same stories. He also provided a good sounding board. I found David to be the way I've found him to be for nearly sixty years: hardheaded, but invaluable.

Lastly, I thank all of you who encouraged me to write this sequel to *Mad Dogs, Marbles, and Rock Fights*. I've had a blast!

www.ingramcontent.com/pod-product-compliance
Lightning Source LLC
Chambersburg PA
CBHW030527080526
44586CB00011B/343